UKULELE

HEROES

Also by Ian Whitcomb

After the Ball: Pop Music from Rag to Rock
(Allen Lane The Penguin Press, 1972)

Tin Pan Alley: A Pictorial History
(Paddington Press, 1975)

LotusLand: A Story of Southern California
(Wildwood House, 1979)

Whole Lotta Shakin: A Rock 'n' Roll Scrapbook
(Arrow Books, 1982)

Rock Odyssey: A Chronicle of the Sixties
(Doubleday Dolphin, 1983)

Irving Berlin & Ragtime America
(Century, 1987)

Resident Alien
(Century, 1990)

The Beckoning Fairground: Notes of a British Exile
(California Classics, 1994)

Letters from Lotusland: An Englishman in Exile
(Wild Shore Press, 2009)

UKULELE

HEROES

THE GOLDEN AGE

IAN WHITCOMB

Edited by Ronny S. Schiff

Hal Leonard Books
An Imprint of Hal Leonard Corporation

Published in 2012 by Hal Leonard Books
An Imprint of Hal Leonard Corporation
7777 West Bluemound Road
Milwaukee, WI 53213

Trade Book Division Editorial Offices
33 Plymouth St., Montclair, NJ 07042

All images are from the author's collection unless otherwise noted.

Printed in the United States of America

Book design by Damien Castaneda

Library of Congress Cataloging-in-Publication Data

Whitcomb, Ian, 1941-
  Ukulele heroes : the golden age / Ian Whitcomb ; edited by Ronny S. Schiff.
      p. cm.
  Includes bibliographical references and index.
  ISBN 978-1-4584-1654-4 (pbk.)
  1. Ukulele players--Biography. I. Schiff, Ronny S. II. Title.
  ML399.W53 2012
  787.8'90922--dc23
  [B]
                        2012013950

www.halleonardbooks.com

For Regina, whose voice sings the sweetest

To firm ukulele accompaniment:

Have a martini,
Put two olives in.
Don't be a meany—
Fill it up to the brim.
Whether it's vodka
Or whether it's gin—
Have a martini
And let life begin!

Oliver De Cologne

I only wish I could!

Ian Whitcomb

CONTENTS

UKULELE HEROES

THE GOLDEN AGE

CHAPTER ONE

A UKULELE SUNDAY

Here in my writing room at the very back of the garden, shaded by an ancient Californian pine, guarded by odd and nameless shrubs, I am in a blissful state of quietude. Why, I could be safe in the old Hawaiian myth-dream!

Away from silently screaming websites mad to inform on matters hitherto unknown to me and thus unimportant, I can calmly tick-tock away on this old computer to tell you the story of the glorious individuals who made ukulele history. Men and women, ranging back to the 1880s, armed with nothing more than four strings in a curvy wooden box, which when struck create a pleasing springy plangency. Un-electric, unobtrusive, and without political or social agenda, these people are my people, my heroes.

Simple artists who delight and hurt not. Some of them beam down from the walls of this writing room helping me keep calm and carry on . . .

Beaver-bucktoothed George Formby from Lancashire (later to be Beatle country), with strong piercing eyes and mile-wide smile, banjo-uke at the ready for high-speed syncopated figures to a rag-catchy tune, crackly un-American voice about to tell of more adventures of Mr. Wu, the laundryman whose eyes wobble while ironing ladies' underwear. Cheshire cat-grinning Tessie O'Shea, full of fun and fatness, with her very own banjo-uke, proudly declaring her closeness to Two Ton Tessie from Tennessee, the gal who lets men play tennis on her double chins. Raccoon-eyed Cliff Edwards, aka Ukulele Ike, with Jazz Age well-scatted novelties about hot babies tempered by poignant departing loves and crowned by his Jiminy Cricket in a far blue yonder promising contentment when we wish upon a star.

At the end of his troubled life, Cliff Edwards, broke and largely forgotten, was interviewed for a "Whatever Happened To . . . ?" book. When asked for a photo he excused himself and went to a cupboard. Out came a bashed-up uke and in came a brave grin and a ready-for-action pose complete with crumpled hat at a jaunty angle.

It's three o'clock—time to go to my own hiding place and pull out a couple of ukes for the regular Sunday night gig at Cantalini's Salerno Beach Restaurant in Playa del Rey by the seaside and next to L.A's International Airport.

For a decade now, I've played with Fred Sokolow (guitar) and Dave Jones (bass) in a corner, as the diners order, eat and chat, and sometimes make discreet love. I use a balalaika-shaped Fluke for the ballads and a metal Johnson, made in China, for the rhythm numbers. And for certain songs, those that need an urgency or brightness, I open up a case to reveal a really jumbo banjo-uke. I love this fellow and have named him "Big Ben": he has a plink-plank that cuts through any excessive restaurant chatter—diners stop open-mouthed with forkfuls of pasta poised midway and quivering. Big Ben's head—at the top, beyond the pegs—is ingrained with a signature: "George Formby." I adore him and the feeling is mutual.

Safe in our corner, we sit and play songs of our choice and to our hearts' content. The planes roar and so do the bikers, while we satisfy Ann, the middle-aged Elvis Lady in the beehive who always tips us $20, with a set of her idol's numbers: "Blue Suede Shoes" and even "Are You Lonesome Tonight?" work well to uke accompaniment.

Is there nothing that can't be strummed on four strings? We have done "The Trout" by Franz Schubert and "In Dreams" by Roy Orbison. Babes in arms are brought close to study the action while we are awarded a view at a nearby table of a girl in low-slung jeans, so low that her leather thong is visible. Is this art? Is this work? Is this where the uke has brought me?

Ten o'clock at night: on the drive home to the San Gabriel Valley, Dave, the bass player, starts a diatribe about people's apathy concerning current affairs in general. But even though his gestures are expansive and his voice stentorian, my mind has wandered to pleasanter fields where alohas blow. And from there to practical matters such as how to get new tuning pegs for my beloved Martin uke so that it doesn't keep going so foully sour.

Ian with "Ukie."

"Ukie" is my prize and I try to only put him through his paces at recordings or special occasions (like when I'm playing for the art deco chanteuse Janet Klein, who wants a certain period look). Ukie is a Martin soprano bought brand new by me at a time when the company was still making heart-meltingly mellifluous instruments. He has some rosewood in him, and he sleeps in a hardshell case lined in plush like a coffin. I paid $350 for him at Wallich's Music City in Hollywood in 1967, when the din of rock and folk-rock was all around and heavy metal was banging at the gate (and our editor, Ronny Schiff, was managing the sheet music department). His sound was considered an old joke by the masses before Tiny Tim came along a little later to turn the joke into a belly laugh.

In the 1970s, Ukie supported me nobly in my first appearance on *The Tonight Show*, and even though Johnny Carson beamed a perplexed look to the millions at home, he did invite me back.

I took Ukie with me to Nashville when I was helping to produce country music for Warner Bros. Records. There he sat among macho pickers and soon he was sweetening up their burliness like a robin in hard and cruel snow.

My fellow producer, an Englishman not under my charm spell, was unimpressed and said after I'd demonstrated a violent narrative ballad to our star vocalist: "I'd like to grab that miserable little object and smash it over your head!"

In those days, the instrument was the very antithesis of cool. Ukie and I were alone against the world. He was my child and ideal friend and I have to admit I abused him. There have been times, in my excitement onstage, when I have swung him against a mike stand or dropped him or bashed him against my head . . .

Dave's lecture on current affairs stops when we reach his home. The rest of the trip, back to my own Altadena home, is spent ruminating: I ought to be more aware of what's going on in the real world and what I can do to help. I ought to stop living in a parallel universe.

And from here, I climb into the sky to consider unknown lights, drifting stars in interstellar conflagrations, primordial ooze floating in space, black holes with the answer deep inside to the meaning of life. Perhaps enthroned at the end of it all is a ukulele ready to tell us that this is what the string theory is all about, this is the answer—in one strum of "My Dog Has Fleas."

At home, and looking myself up on YouTube in case there's a new entry—some funny number caught by the iPhone of a fan at an obscure coffeehouse gig—I stumble on news from the new world of radical alternative ukes and I am brought down to earth with a bump.

I already know from a mere scanning of newspapers and magazines that today ukuleles are suddenly everywhere. No longer are they, says *Rolling Stone*, novelties, mere toys. Taylor Swift wields one, Train made the Top 10 with "Hey, Soul Sister," and Eddie Vedder, once a

noisy noisome Pearl Jammer, has made an entire album with just the four strings, while soaring away to outer space (stopping en route for a concert-hall date with a few classical fellows) is Jake Shimabukuro with a virtuoso sound light-years from cheerful George Formby.

But whereas Ukulele Ike and George Formby had no trouble cradling their instruments fondly and carefully, as if holding a baby, these rockers look awkward without big and threatening guitars. They haven't yet worked out the cool moves, the attack stance, the way Jimi would work the picture with the little fellow. Complains one old Australian rocker: "The bloody thing makes me look like an effing gorilla playing with his dong!"

Now as I go online tonight come challenges to fever up my mind from websites that offer ukulele revolution, a way to bring change to a corrupt world, to deal with Wall Street and the overrich and on the way, perhaps, cover a few songs by the Clash, the Undertones, Pulp, Arctic Monkeys. One thing is clear, screams RevYuke: the old comfortable borders that once defined uke music will be wiped off the map! "We are the future and there'll be no singalongs!!" shouts Ratfinkuke. "With U bro!!!" says Fuxxx2U, adding a defaced photo of poor Tiny Tim.

I go to bed determined to get back to the beginnings, to show that my Ukie and Big Ben have an uninterrupted time line, a continuum, a rich historical pageant peopled by a peaceful army of heroes, marching to the old, old melodic and rhythmic story, and ready, at the end of the road, to welcome me and my ukes to our place in the glorious golden age.

We need to return to the islands. To Hawai'i . . .

Queen Lili'uokalani.
Courtesy of the Hawai'i State Archives.

From the collection of Flea Market Music.

CHAPTER TWO

A GIFT FROM THE ISLANDS

HAWAIIAN BEGINNINGS

Hawai'i in the popular mind: a siren to the world-weary, a pleasure spot where anything goes, amid swaying palms and sun-drenched beaches facing a coral sea scented by the fragrance of strange flowers and decorated by the sensuous swaying of grass-skirted, well-rounded brown maids with hula hands and hula hips and everything in the line of temptations. And look! One of these maids is leaning against an engorged and weird tree and she's strumming a ukulele.

This enticing image was a long time in the making. Local businessmen, with help from Mainland writers like

Mark Twain and Jack London, plus a flurry of anonymous publicists, worked hard at the creation of an Edenic paradise only a boat trip away. The fact that by the 1880s native Hawaiians were a minority was not allowed to interfere with the myth of bronzed boys and curvy gals. Music played an important role, with ukuleles and steel guitars pointing up the exoticism. However, it was a very different music scene in 1778, when Captain Cook discovered what Twain later described as "the loveliest fleet of islands anchored in any ocean."

Cook was welcomed to what he called his Sandwich Isles by a sacred but rather monotonous chant. The indigenous Polynesian music tradition, without tune or harmony, was percussive: leaving aside the odd nose flute and eerie chanting, it was sticks on stones, some gnarly rattles, and a slapping of the chest and thighs—all in the name of the spiritual rather than the sensual. The repetitive welcome concert went on and on till the captain grew bored. It was a pity that he was murdered and dismembered by the islanders before he could enjoy a proper religious hula demonstration by bare-chested local girls.

Straight-backed Congregationalist missionaries from icy New England put a stop to any more of this hula nonsense. From the 1820s, they sailed in and installed their ways. The voluminous Mother Hubbard housedress (or mu'u mu'u) covered the seminaked women while their menfolk were introduced to the pleasures and practicalities of the trouser. On the plus side, the natives were taught reading and writing, and this included music—of the "right" sort.

Soon the congregations were singing the rather stern and chilling hymns soaringly. A peculiar sweetness and a tendency to sing high and with much vibrato was noted and encouraged, especially after the introduction of the Spanish guitar by imported South American cowboys called in to help with the otherwise ignored cattle. The grown-up children of the missionaries leapt into lay life with a vengeance, buying up land, running the sugar plantations, getting things done in a hurry—as certain Western civilizations are prone to do. The natives watched, catching the fruit as it fell from the trees and the fish as they leapt into their laps, while the new Christian Hawaiians, the haoles, brought in hordes of Chinese and Japanese to work the sugar fields.

There was diversion from all this hard work ethic. Hawaiian royalty, descended from high chiefs who in turn were descended from the gods, became plenty interested in the European music floating from the Westerners' houses. In 1870, after a series of ship-band concerts by a visiting Austrian frigate in Honolulu, the citizens of Honolulu demanded from the government their very own band.

Now, this government was based on the British model, with a parliament and a flag like the Union Jack. They even used "God Save the Queen" as the national anthem for a while, until a Prussian anthem with Hawaiian words was substituted. The hereditary monarchy was like the British one, only with even less actual power—figureheads under a constitution written by the "missionary boys." For the cunning and clever haoles were ever so slowly, but quite forcibly, becoming the controllers of the business side of the pleasure islands. After all, income had to come from somewhere, otherwise the game was up. The white economists reckoned it might as well be sugar—and other things yet to be planted and exploited. Let the haoles run the day-to-day business and leave the good times to native royalty.

King Kamehameha V applied to the German government for a bandmaster, and the Kaiser obliged with a pedagogue called Captain Henry (Heinrich in his homeland) Berger who arrived in Honolulu in 1872. The king didn't mince words about the difficulties the captain might have with the locals. He talked of their ignorance of discipline and their tendency to wander off beachwards. "Then I'll lock them in a dark room," laughed Berger, an easygoing man for a Prussian officer. The king, who'd been around, said: "They'll like that; they'll sleep all day. Take a stick to them. That is the only way." And he presented the new bandleader with a stout shillelagh given to him by a recent Irish immigrant. Berger never used it, but later confessed that he had to be pretty strict to get his wards to blow the brass instruments in the proper manner. Nevertheless the Royal Hawaiian Band grew to be quite a natty outfit and was later used by the government to welcome tourists to the islands.

Luckily, Berger had a musically open mind and a desire to tap into any local talent. He listened to and transcribed native tunes he heard at luaus and church gatherings; he recognized the unique loveliness of the Hawaiian voice and the natural languor of the islanders. For every Germanic march he added to the Royal Band's repertoire, he'd balance it with his arrangement of a native tune or hula. He fell in love with the local culture and made it his mission to package it for world presentation.

In the royal court—while nearby, in hot but well-appointed offices, the white businessmen got on with business—Berger encour-aged as much music-making as possible. He approved of Prince Leleiohoku's II slightly lubricious love song "We Two in the Spray" (the melody of the song is known as "The Hawaiian War Chant"). He listened attentively as Lydia Lili'uokalani, wife of Boston Brahmin-born John Owen Dominis and also a princess in her own right, performed her latest song at the piano, and he put up with her brother David's fooling on guitar, mandolin, or accordion.

When David was made King Kalakaua in 1874, the court became a riot of melody and dance. The hula was reinstated, and there was much twisting and twirling and churning. Real French champagne lubricated the party. Publicly, the king threw an extravagant two-week birthday party where for one day all the bands and groups played at once and Captain Berger held his head in his hands but smiled; this was

From the collection of Flea Market Music.

One of the many printed versions of "Aloha Oe" sheet music.
From the collection of Flea Market Music.

followed by a luau for ten thousand guests and hangers-on. Eight years later Kalakaua had a proper coronation, a very expensive affair, in front of the spanking new and shiny 'Iolani Palace, built at a cost of $350,000. Government officials took note and there were grumblings and rumblings. Some discussed the overthrow of this heedless and hedonistic Merry Monarch.

However, there was a quieter and more reflective side to King David. He found time to write tender love songs, which were then arranged for his glee club. He tried to keep up with his sister's stream of compositions, but he lacked her formal training, perfect pitch, and single-minded devotion. Songs could strike Princess Lili'uokalani anywhere and down they'd be jotted or held in the head by constant humming till music paper could be produced.

Inspiration came to her on horseback in 1877 when she was at the Boyd Ranch and espied an intense good-bye clinch between Colonel James Harbottle Boyd, who ought to have known better, and a comely young stable girl. Friends aided Lili'uokalani in her humming on the ride back, and soon everybody was joining in the creative process. One of the men congratulated her on such a good new use of the hymn "The Lone Rock by the Sea." Someone else pointed out that the melody echoed an old European folk song. Then an American guest pointed out the closeness to pop songwriter Freddie Root's "There's Music in the Air." The princess wasn't fazed. She'd make something new out of this now-orphaned hum.

When she got home to Washington Place, she fashioned what was to be the great Hawaiian farewell song, "Aloha 'Oe." Henry Berger arranged it for brass band, and the song was played for decades by his Royal Hawaiian Band as tourist boats steamed out of Honolulu Bay.

But it sounded more tender, more wrenchingly nostalgic when accompanied by an odd but winning new instrument introduced by indentured foreigners to the islands in 1879.

A baby guitar with only four strings but a great plunk.

The king was to go wild about the baby and had to have and hold and play. The princess was more restrained and dubbed it "the gift that came here"—a gift (*uku*) that came (*lele*) all the way from Madeira, a cluster of Portuguese-owned islands off the Moroccan coast.

In sunny Portugal, Britain's oldest ally and the source of her corner on the sherry market, there's a town called Braga. In the 1700s

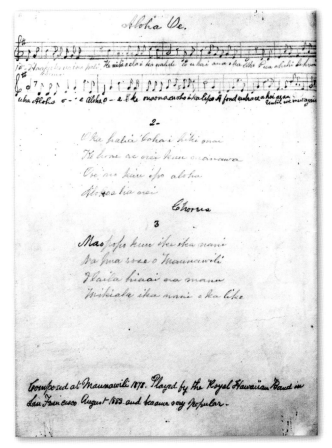

ingly novel versions of the latest gems from the richly upholstered ballrooms where fashion thronged. With a large enough tip, maybe the peasants could answer a request for an operatic air request or a Chopin étude? How amusing! How exotic!

There were dissenters. A visitor, one Senator Dix of New York, felt that the machete was weak and needed help. In his 1850 travel book *A Winter in Madeira and a Summer in Spain and Florence*, he wrote: "Its music, by itself, is thin and meagre; but in the streets at night, with a guitar or violin-cello accompaniment, it is very pretty." And what is the point of *machete* melody picking when the music would sound much better on a guitar ("[i]n all respects a finer instrument")? This criticism was to haunt the history of the *machete* as it metamorphosed into the ukulele, and is still relevant today in the concert clang and clash of the Great Revival. Do we, for example, need "Rhapsody in Blue" on the uke? Or "The Flight of the Bumblebee"?

Hawai'i's business corps, in the process of buying up the sugarcane plantations, badly needed laborers. From 1878 and over the next decade, thousands were recruited and many came from Madeira. On August 23, 1879, the British ship *Ravenscrag* deposited 423 men,

the locals could be heard playing a little four-string guitar they called the *machete de braga* to distinguish it from rival baby guitars like the *cavaquinho* and the *rajão*. Guitars lent a little depth to the plink-plank, and there was a certain amount of singing and perhaps dancing. No big thing.

However, across the sea, in Madeira, the stunted imp caught on and by mid-1800s was the pop hit of the country. Well-dressed visitors were impressed by street performances by peasant riffraff and the like. A tiny simpleton, but in the right hands pleasing harmonies floated out across the square as accompaniment to rude singers who rendered fascinat-

women, and children from the island onto another island, Oʻahu, but one with more opportunities. The indentured workers were overjoyed to be in Hawaiʻi and one of them, a kid called João Fernandes, in his glee jumped down from the ship and started singing Portuguese folk songs while accompanying himself on the *machete*. The locals were entranced by the music of the little guitar. Two weeks later the *Hawaiian Gazette* reported that a band of Portuguese musicians "have been delighting the people with nightly street concerts." They play "strange instruments which are a kind of cross between a guitar and a banjo." The music was considered "very sweet" and it was hoped there'd be more.

Here was a sound for the song of islands, one that fitted nicely into the Anglo-Hawaiian tradition of satisfying rock-steady Protestant hymnody and the rich German harmonies of the ballads and marches made and taught by Captain Berger.

Just as the missionary boys had their moneymaking fields, so the cannier Portuguese visitors soon had their own business too. After their contracts were fulfilled and their hands washed free of plantation soil, three Ravenscraggers decided to get into cabinetmaking, with stringed instruments as a side business. After all, they were, in truth, not field hands but skilled artist-artisans. And local interest in the *machete* meant there might be sales in the offing. Manuel Nunes, Jose do Espirito Santo, and Augusto Dias independently opened shops stocked with furniture and also, as a diversion, *machetes* and the five-string *rajãos*. By common consent these were labeled "taro-patch fiddles"—something you strummed for a bit of fun in the vegetable patch. A little more refine-

ment for easier playing after serious public interest and there emerged what we would recognize as the modern ukulele. Strum it and you'd hear the familiar "My Dog Has Fleas" tune.

There is another claimant for the coining of the word "ukulele." I've told how Princess Liliʻuokalani dreamed up the gift-from-afar idea, but here's another and more colorful origin tale. For this we return to the mad magic of the Merry Monarch's court: Augusto Dias, one of the original Ravenscraggers, insinuated himself into King David's circle after word got around that this Dias was a pretty picker. Soon he was gigging in the comfy bungalow at the fabulous ʻIolani Palace, egged on by David for more and madder music and plied with champagne as the king and his cronies played poker and lived it up. The king took a few lessons and became passable in his own excited manner, but his sister noted the tenderness of the *machete* and made musical note. Perhaps Captain Berger could incorporate the little child into one of his native ensembles?

The real talent at the court gatherings was a rather sleek and slimy British army officer called Edward Purvis. He made sure he didn't do his *machete* act till after the princess had said goodnight. Expelled from Sandhurst—the top-hole military college and training ground for future enforcers of British Empire rule—for conduct unbecoming an officer and gentleman, black sheep Purvis headed for Hawaiʻi believing it to be a British colony. There he wangled his way into the court, persuading the Anglophile and easily impressed King David—who loved card tricks—to appoint him assistant chamberlain. Like many con men, he was fast on the uptake, and after watching Dias at the parties and limiting his champagne intake, Purvis became a damn decent *machete* player and was often called upon to give closed concerts.

He was a little man with a tendency to nervously wriggle his body, shake his shoulders, and waggle his head as he did an Irish jig or sang a lewd British music-hall song to his *machete* accompaniment. So the courtesans, led by the king, nicknamed him "Ukulele," which can be translated as a jumping, leaping or bouncing flea. David used to snap his fingers and say, "Ukulele! Give us that song about sherry wine and the damsel!"

In the dry light of day, a sober king was informed by Mr. Gibson, his trusted prime minister, that Purvis was sneaking gory details of the bungalow parties to the capitalists in government, men eager to find an excuse to dethrone the monarch. More than that, Purvis published an anonymous scandal sheet describing his boss as a boozing, philandering, aboriginal idiot. Why, the king was no more than the son of a Negro servant! Purvis was fired and left the islands in disgrace.

But there was no stopping the rot. In 1887, sister Lydia was enjoying a visit to Buckingham Palace and meeting Queen Victoria when she heard the news about her feeble brother caving in to political pressure by signing away much of his power, on threat of execution, to the businessmen: the so-called Bayonet Constitution. Lili'uokalani cut short her tour and hurried home.

There was little left of the monarchy when her brother, on one of his many West Coast trips, died in San Francisco in 1891. The new Queen Lili'uokalani was warned and consoled by the king's widow, Queen Kapi'olani, in a song she'd specially written for her husband's return which now took on a foreboding air.

Accompanying herself on a ukulele made for her by the Ravenscragger Manuel Nunes, Kapi'olani sang "I Have a Feeling of Love," a beautiful ballad that likens her dead lover to a dazzling vermilion native bird, the honeycreeper, a creature in danger of extinction. The bell was tolling for old Hawai'i and native Hawaiians.

The new queen's reign didn't last long. The United States was in an expansionist mood, the search for colonies was infecting all world powers, and besides that, the entire Hawaiian economy, from sugarcane and fruit right down to the splendid electric lights and trolley cars, was the result of American know-how and go-aheadness. Neither the Japanese nor the British, forever nosing around Honolulu in their ships, should have this gleaming lush prize.

In 1893 a Committee of Safety led by Americans and Europeans executed a coup d'état. The queen made sure it was bloodless before surrendering her throne to "the superior forces of the United States"—referring to a hundred or so U.S. Marines and sailors who'd marched in. Sanford Dole, leader of the overthrow group and a descendant of Protestant missionaries from Maine, was made president of the new republic, later to be annexed by the United States. His young nephew Jim would soon be ready to start a fruit canning empire, where he'd become "The Pineapple King" and Scott Joplin would write a rag in celebration.

Meanwhile, the queen had spent some prison time, but she used it wisely to write a touching "Queen's Prayer." After her pardon, she lived quietly at home in Washington Place in Honolulu, continuing to make music: "My only consolation, as natural as breathing and the tick of the heart."

Captain Berger visited her often to make

music, and the two shared organ chores at Kawaiahaʻo Church. Berger had suffered during the day of the usurpation: looters had torn stamps from envelopes in his files, and ceremonial buttons were ripped from his uniforms. A man who believed in stability and an establishment as well as common-sense compromise, he'd accepted the new provisional government while keeping up his friendship with the queen.

He became a patcher-upper, a forgive-and-forgetter: in 1914 he managed to persuade the old queen to sit on the same platform as her nemesis Sanford Dole at a celebration of Hawaiian culture—near the party bungalow in the grounds of the ʻIolani Palace where once ukuleles and high joyous voices rang out against the clink of champagne flutes. The official photograph shows nobody smiling.

But Dole, now ex-territorial governor and loving his freedom, made a speech about the importance and influence of Hawaiian music in the world. It was understood by all that he was not referring, as he might have done twenty years before, to European-style band music—apologies to Captain Berger—but to the lap steel guitar, the sweet glee singing, and, most of all, to this now-native instrument called "ukulele," pride of the islands, siren to mainlanders to come see our beautiful land.

Since 1889, before the troubles, the ukulele had been recognized as the national instrument. It had come through that unfortunate period unscathed and unattached, a child everyone wanted to adopt. The queen played one, of course; Dole had just bought a concert model especially made for him by M. Nunes ("Inventor of the original Ukulele," as his ads claimed, and what's more, "Patronized by the Royal Hawaiian Family"). Even the captain, swallowing

his pride, had promised to try at his earliest opportunity. He was quick to mention that one of his bandsmen, Major Kealakai, had already gone and gotten published a ukulele and taro-patch instruction book by a noted Los Angeles music company. Oh, yes, he would definitely study the little thing.

If Hawaiʻi was to present itself as a world-class player, then the ukulele was its best ambassador!

ⓖⓖⓖⓖⓖⓖⓖⓖ

On the platform at the celebration, with the captain between them as peacemaker, Queen Lydia Liliʻuokalani and Sanford Dole look stiff and uneasy, and yet the picture symbolizes the new and long-term alliance of the songsters and ukesters with the merchants and businessmen. Both parties were in the business of selling Hawaiian product whether it be hula or pineapple. The sooner the stuff reached the mainland, the better.

Meanwhile, there were visitors to beckon in and welcome. Constant boatloads were offered leis, grass skirts, and even poi (if kept securely boxed), together with hand-tinted color postcards and sheet music from local publishers and songwriters—souvenirs to carry home carefully to Pasadena or even Des Moines as the boat shuddered off from the bay to the strains of Berger's band playing a farewell "Aloha ʻOe." A song long stripped of any vestiges of sadness or regret, and now a harmless lullaby rocking the tourists into the sleep of all's well in the world, and clean as a whistle too, as all American history should be.

Left in Honolulu, but working as hard as their peers in New York's Tin Pan Alley, were

Written by Sonny Cunha and published by the Bergstrom Music Company.
From the collection of Rick Cunha.

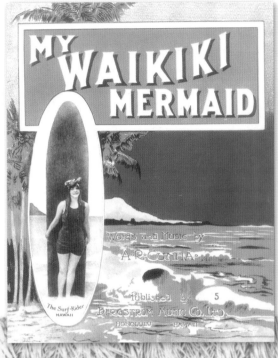

A Sonny Cunha 1915 postcard that he handed out while running for the Territorial House of Representatives; note he is using his uke as a campaign gimmick.
From the collection of Rick Cunha.

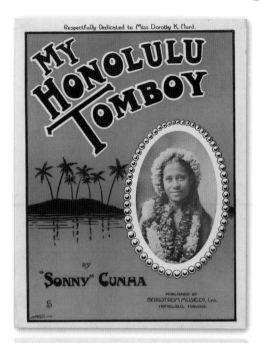

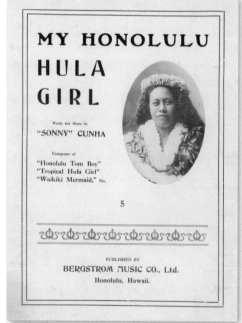

The lyrics in these songs were quite sexually charged in Hawaiian double entendre; check them out.

From the online collection of Rick Cunha.

music publishers such as the Bergstrom Music Company and songwriters such as Albert R. "Sonny" Cunha.

Sonny was the canniest of the lot, a Yale Law School graduate who, having gifted his alma mater with their anthem "Boola Boola," based on a hula tune, returned to his native country to practice raggy hula rather than tricky torts. Cunha savvied that there might be a market for island songs if written in the current ragtime style—syncopated, sassy, and peppered with Hawaiian words for seasoning up the Alley English. Simple, catchy tunes perfect for ukulele accompaniment, with a distinctive "vamp" or "turnaround" musical phrase that later became a trademark of Hawaiian song. His "My Honolulu Tomboy" (1905) and "Hapa Haole Hula Girl" (1909) were up-to-date maids who sported about in the backseats of autos. "Hapa haole" meant half-white, like Cunha himself, who was proud to be of Portuguese extraction.

His contemporary, but not necessarily his friend, was Charles E. King, a rather rigid bearded composer and ragtime-despiser who had been taught by Queen Liliʻuokalani herself. Graduating in the first class from the Kamehameha School for Boys and speaking perfect Hawaiian, King went on to be a conscientious preserver of island music while developing a romantic sort of outdoorsy parlor song style, full of barbershop harmony but always worded in the native tongue. His work was later Americanized, given lyrics, and he landed huge hits in "Song of the Islands" and "The Hawaiian Wedding Song." Being a traditionalist, he would never have approved of such tampering. Like Sonny Cunha, he was only fractionally native, but we must remember that full-bloodied Hawaiians were a minority and that this U.S. territory was being peopled by many races, including a considerable number of Asians.

Cunha and King music was stay-at-home. No hits as yet. But meanwhile ukuleles were already on the road abroad trying stir up interest and dollars.

Roving bands of Hawaiians with lap guitars, taro-patches, and ukuleles had been making inroads in America since the 1890s. There were ukulele players at the 1893 World's Columbian Exposition in Chicago, accompanying the Volcano Singers. They might well have witnessed Scott Joplin playing his ragtime piano somewhere in the midway, or taken a few pointers from the sensational Little Egypt and her lascivious but immensely watchable hoochie-coochie dance.

In the next decade or so, other Hawaiian troupes spread out across the USA, appearing in educational tent shows in Buffalo, as supporting acts in vaudeville shows on the Keith circuit, at blue-blooded affairs at Harvard, and eventually before President Taft and his guest, a Chinese prince, at a state dinner at the White House in 1910. Attention at all these events was polite; the novelty was acknowledged. There was no sensation. That would start next year.

At bottom, it was the exotic image of dusky lusty lads and well-rounded maids from a faraway place where clothing was optional and conduct could be unbecoming that appealed to the heavily clothed and morally strictured mainlanders, even as they bounced about to turkey trots played by a ragtime band. In 1911 and onward, it was the turn of the Hawaiians to captivate and titillate America and the world, and to give ragtime a run for its money.

The image was perfectly captured and pro-

jected via *The Bird of Paradise*, a lurid melodramatic romance dreamed up by a mainlander playwright from San Francisco called Richard Walton Tully and first staged in Los Angeles to an excited audience in the autumn of 1911. Impresario Oliver Morosco was bankrolled by San Francisco mayor James Phelan—and one Claus Spreckels, a German-American industrialist who, since the 1880s, had controlled the Hawaiian sugar business and would have controlled the islands (he was nicknamed "His Majesty" by the inhabitants), had he not been outwitted by King Kalakaua in one of the monarch's rare bursts of cleverness. Sitting on the fence during the overthrow of the monarchy, Spreckels watched the subsequent growth of the tourist industry with interest from his San Francisco office, taking time out to enjoy the music of the newly resident local Hawaiian string band and even hiring them for his parties.

Despite the fact that one of the archvillains in *The Bird of Paradise* was a rapacious sugar baron, Spreckels realized there were elements in the play that could gratify the senses, even tickle the groin and, if there was nonstop background string music from steel guitars and ukuleles, the production might drum up business for the steamship line in which he'd invested.

Indeed, the play had everything in the line of box-office boffo: a white American boy in a steamy romance with a Hawaiian princess, a nasty missionary and the aforesaid sugar baron as villains, an angry volcano that erupted spectacularly, and then the climax, when the heroine, victim of doomed love, threw herself into the fiery crater. Naked passion and sacred gods; sex and religion—a safe bet for success.

But beyond the old story of forbidden fruit

was the fresh sound, like a line of wobbly waves, provided by the incidental music of a five-piece native band featuring two ukuleles and a lap slide guitar all the way from Hawai'i. Or were they chosen by Spreckels from his pool of San Francisco party boys?

The sell-out show went out for a little tour before opening on Broadway in 1912, where the *New York Times* critic remarked on "the weirdly sensuous music of the Island people." Again, the play hit the bull's-eye even as the nation was in thrall to the clarion call of Irving Berlin's smash hit "Alexander's Ragtime Band." You certainly couldn't wriggle and jiggle at a furious pace to the weird new island music, but the body also needs the juicy fruit of the sexy slow drag, and the Hawaiians provided that in spades. The show's Hawaiian Quintette, seen onstage in a sylvan setting, were recorded by Victor Records, who chose to have them play "Tomi Tomi," the tale of a girl who likes to be manhandled by her lover. Sales were brisk. *The Bird of Paradise* went on to tour the nation and then Europe for many years.

Now the Hawaiian craze started building and not just with tourists landing in Honolulu. On the West Coast, there was a lot of action: the son of one of the Ravenscraggers, Leo Nunes, set up shop to sell ukuleles in Los Angeles, while in San Francisco the Hawaiian-born Keech brothers sold ukes and method books. Responding to this, Sears, Roebuck and Co., the retail giant straddling the entire land, advertised ukuleles in its fall 1914 catalog with the come-on comment that "the ukulele is creating a sensation in this country, especially on the Pacific Coast, where it is exceedingly popular."

But what really turned the sensation into a long-lasting phenomenon of several years was the Panama-Pacific International Exposition held in San Francisco in 1915.

The Hawaiian government knew a good thing when they saw it, and the legislature appropriated $100,000 for the erection of a Hawaiian Building at the expo to show off what the new U.S territory had to offer. Strange, dazzling fish and flora were popular, but it was the daily music shows that gained the most attention from the seventeen million who attended the exposition. Hawai'i had sent across its top musicians, headed by a house band led by Keoki Awai and his Royal Hawaiian Quartet, smiling lads all in white and with leis round their necks, showing off a lap guitar and an eight-string ukulele, together with the regular soprano model.

They played in the main pavilion in a gazebo filled with flowers, while other groups played the Hawaiian Village and the gardens, with hula girls flitting from venue to venue, intoxicating a public craving a new sensation in popular music. One reporter observed that in the tropical gardens, "the canaries have heard the music so often that at certain times they take up the tune and sing the accompaniment." Others strained to describe the otherworldly sounds that seemed minor, but were in fact major made sad and reflective by the sinuous swoops of the steel guitar and the shimmer strum of the ukes. Then the reporters' eyes again darted to the athletic moves of the hula girls, hips rotating seductively in what was described in the program as a sacred religious exercise—looked like the old bump-and-grind to the press boys.

If all this distraction was not enough, there were concession booths where gaily singing and bellowing island entrepreneurs sold their wares. Jonah Kumalae stood like a vol-

This consummate collection has served as the bible of Hawaiian songs for over 100 years.

From the collection of Flea Market Music.

A GIFT FROM THE ISLANDS

Respectfully Dedicated
to MARTA GOLDEN

ON THE BEACH AT WAIKIKI

OR THE

GOLDEN HULA

WORDS BY
G. H. STOVER

5

Arranged by
"SONNY" CUNHA

MUSIC BY
HENRY KAILIMAI

Published by
Sherman, Clay & Co.
SAN FRANCISCO.

cano above the rest: a prominent politician on the Honolulu Board of Supervisors, he also manufactured the best poi. At his booth, he was surrounded by fine homemade ukuleles and taro-patches, as well as leis made out of fresh flowers and calabash, a rather tough but ultimately tasty fruit.

So naturally the hustling islanders were not happy to find themselves jostled in their concession rows by interlopers with their mainland-made instruments, method books, and sheet music. Some of these wares were mislabeled as "Made in Hawai'i." The Keech brothers, Alvin and Kelvin, were almost acceptable, because, despite being the sons of a Pennsylvanian, they'd grown up in Hawai'i. But here they were armed with product and, like young Frankensteins, full of ideas for the future manufacturing of hybrid ukes—such as fusing on a mandolin or banjo.

The racket from the hucksters was like a convention of auto salesmen. When it could be heard above the din, Henry Kailimai's deep, almost operatic voice performing his song "On the Beach at Waikiki" eventually became the hum of the expo. With a characteristic mix of Hawaiian and English lyrics by a Dr. Stover and a piano arrangement by Sonny Cunha, the number was the first hapa haole hit. Back in Honolulu, the Bergstrom Music Company was very pleased and the presses rolled.

Kailimai's song was played frequently by the Hawaiian spin-off bands, some native and some not, that fanned out over the USA after the expo ended. Vaudeville and Chautauqua circuits welcomed them, and audiences were mesmerized until the coming of the next sensation—jazz. Bands like the North Carolina Hawaiians were big in the South, where kids wowed to the steel guitar and so took it to their hearts that they made it their own when hillbilly music became "country and western." Some age-old but stirring folk memory welled up to wash the wavering feather-light song of the islands into the deep mud of the Mississippi.

But it was hard shellac and printed paper that stamped Hawaiian music into the consciousness of Americans needing constant diversion. East Coast record companies were all releasing Hawaiian numbers by 1916, and they weren't choosy about whether the bands were actually on the islands. If you bought a Victrola, a Hawaiian record was included free, maybe even one of the rare performances captured in field recordings made in Honolulu.

In September of that year, *The Edison Phonograph Monthly* reported on the brisk sales of the new sound: "Two years ago, what did the public know about Hawaiian Music, Ukuleles, Hula Hula Dances? Since then, Hawaiian music and American versions of it have taken the United States by storm." Victor Records claimed the new style, "Hawaiian-American Ragtime," sold more than any other, to the tune of hundreds of thousands of discs. The Martin Guitar Company of Pennsylvania, experimenting in the flush of the expo splash, made a dozen ukes in 1915; by 1917 they were selling two thousand, and after that sales kept leaping. These were quality instruments every bit as tuneful as the island variety.

Tin Pan Alley's take on Hawaiian songs.

From the collection of Flea Market Music.

Refinement and good taste were not attributes of Tin Pan Alley, the song and fun factory in New York where fads were rhymed and set to jingles the moment they surfaced. Taking a breather from Dixie themes, the Alleymen, without leaving their work cubicles, were soon calling in blackface characters from the minstrel era and setting them beside palm trees under a yellow moon: Bill Bailey, last seen being chased down the street in his nightshirt by his irate women, was now smilingly plunking in "When Old Bill Bailey Plays the Ukalele" (note the misspelling). What did the Alleymen care? "Bill . . ." reached No. 16 on the sheet music trade paper chart for January 1916. He was closely followed by "Hello, Hawaii, How Are You?" a long-distance telephone song with a Jewish comic on the cover. "Yaaka Hula Hickey Dula" had a visitor swayed to and played to by a hula maiden in a melody that borrowed from many an old island anthem. It hit No. 1. Then there was "Oh, How She Could Yacki Hacki Wicki Wacki Woo," where you could choose your double entendre, and "They're Wearing 'Em Higher in Hawaii," which was obvious. Poor Henry Kailimai's "On the Beach at Waikiki," hit of the expo, barely scraped into the Top 20.

While ukulele music was indeed the flavor of the day, native garb was being shed. Creamy trousers, curly hair, and beaming milk-chocolate faces gave way to city-slicker vaudevillians in shouting check suits and derbies or striped blazers and straw hats, exchanging canes for ukes at the climax of their act.

After a brief intermission, when the doughboys did their bit in the Great War to songs about beating the Hun, set to a ragtime tune, American pop faced a new craze, which had exploded even as the guns roared over there: jazz. Stunned by million-seller Victor artists the Original Dixieland Jazz Band—five boys from New Orleans blasting cacophony—and by the chaotic bands that copied and followed them, the Alleymen citified their Southern paradise songs and added jazz babies with a touch of the blues: "How Ya Gonna Keep 'Em Down on the Farm" when they crave the "Blues My Naughty Sweetie Gives to Me"? You'd have thought the peaceful little ukulele would have been shoved into the attic. But in the frantic, socially liberating 1920s—Scott Fitzgerald's Jazz Age—the uke became an important part of Flaming Youth's fashion gear.

For it was easier to woo the girl of your dreams with the portable uke than with expensive drums or sax. Besides, the thing was easy to manipulate—the few essential chords might be mastered in an hour or so with the help of one of the many method books. Another advantage over other instruments was that the uke was a hogwash detector: all music was reduced to a few chords and a melody. Fancy arrangements like the ones you heard on natty dance-band records by Paul Whiteman were revealed as pretentious fluff covering up the original tune and harmony when you sat down with the song sheet and uke-analyzed. Helpful publishers would soon be printing chord grids to show you where to press your fingers on the frets for the correct strum. Thus: armed with a stripped-down song and a sexy hourglass-figure mini machine, your young male cake-eater could croon in her ear till ready and then toss the baby on the grass or sand when the time was ripe for action.

If you were too lazy to learn, there were professional uke entertainers at the ready. You could hear them on record clearly enunciating—far better than the blues shouters—and even clearer on the radio. Radio, about to become a home entertainment and rival to records and sheet music, had the benefit of electricity: sensitive microphones that showed up the blunderbuss metal recording horns. The ukulele was dulcet compared with other instruments, and entertainers who came with them were welcomed by the radio executives.

In the blare of the Jazz Age party, then, the ukulele held its own. No longer solely associated with hula maidens under swaying palm trees, our little friend was now firmly established in American show business. In 1926, the Martin Guitar Company sold fourteen thousand, a peak year never to be challenged. Vaudevillian Frank Lane was advertising himself in the trade papers as "one of the few remaining entertainers who work without the aid of a ukulele."

Nevertheless there were now star stylists of the uke proving that it was more than a stage prop, more than a flapper-trapper, more than a pleasant plunk. These stars used the strings as a bed on which to bounce out their distinctive personalities, telling stories that moved the spirit to chuckle one moment and to tear up the next. They painted life with simple but not simplistic strokes. Art without fanfare or pretense. Cliff Edwards—aka "Ukulele Ike"—led these kings. In 1926, he hit with two songs in which he was able to wear both the comic and the tragic mask: "Paddlin' Madelin' Home" and "The Lonesomest Girl in Town."

We move to the realm of the mainland Ukulele Heroes.

HERE I STRAY IT SEEMS •
'NEATH THE DREAMY SUMMER

CHAPTER THREE

THE JAZZ AGE
AND BEYOND

CLIFF EDWARDS—"UKULELE IKE"

"When I was a baby we moved around a bit, but I always personally packed my rattle and milk bottle . . . I never saw the inside of a college . . . In Texas I drove a milk truck through the fence of a game preserve and forty wild buffaloes came after the truck—so I gave it to them . . . They threw me off the stage at the Palace because I made a joke about my strings being the guts of a cat . . . .

"The public doesn't care a hoot about my background as long as it can hear me play the ukulele and see me make funny faces.

"I have no social position. I am just Ukulele Ike."

Always good copy for newspaper and magazines journalists, especially in divorce court or at bankruptcy proceedings, Cliff "Ukulele Ike" Edwards never went high-hat, never got pretentious even though at the height of his career in the 1920s he played the Palace Theatre in New York (mecca of vaudeville) and initiated hits like "Fascinating Rhythm" on Broadway and "Singin' in the Rain" in Hollywood. He also sold millions of records.

In the history of popular music, he was far more important than he'd ever admit.

Today his vocal stylings are considered by critics to be the birth of jazz singing, with their lazy sprawl over the bars and the improvised growls and high wailing to nonsense syllables that later, in the armory of Louis Armstrong and Ella Fitzgerald, were termed "scat." Ike called it "eefin'" or just plain "fuckin' aroun'." After all, jazz was another word for that same force of nature.

Accompanied quite often by jazz bands, Cliff Edwards was at his purest when alone with his uke (not an instrument approved of by jazz purists), crooning, jazzing, making odd noises supported by a nimble strumming in which exactly the right string was singled out from the strummed chord to complement the vocal and prevent any monotony. A skill such as no other ukester before him had displayed. But once again Edwards became Mr. Modest. In 1927 the star was asked to define his work tool, his "lamb chop," as his pals called it: "A modern instrument for those who don't care to spend many hours in study," he replied.

As far as the three Rs were concerned, Clifton A. Edwards had never really made their acquaintance, because his mind was on higher matters.

Here are the facts of his life, with some interpolations where the holes are . . .

He was born on a houseboat in Hannibal, Missouri, on June 14, 1895. His father, Edward, was a railroad man, working the caboose at the rear of a freight train. His mother, Nellie, worked the home, singing the songs of the day to stay bright. Cliff loved them both. When he was ten and his father was too ill to work, he got a job stamping the company name on the heels of shoes made by the Rand shoe company, a local outfit. His fellow workers enjoyed the a cappella concerts he'd give them where he'd veer from the humor of "A Woman Is Only a Woman, But a Good Cigar Is a Smoke" to a tearjerker like "Your Mother Wants You Home, Boy."

One day, when he was on his rounds selling newspapers (he also painted freight cars and sold magazines subscriptions to make ends meet), he stopped at the Mark Twain Hotel, where Twain himself, who'd been born in Hannibal as Sam Clemens, was holding a press conference on the front porch. The celebrity liked to return to the old hometown and yarn. The boy tried to have a word with the great man, but all he got was a wink and "No speakee!" That was a big event for the boy in this sleepy burg where they rolled up the sidewalks at seven o'clock.

At age fourteen Cliff went on the road for several years. Money was sent home to support his ailing parents. In St. Louis, a hotbed of classic ragtime, he sang in saloons for tips. Miss Lily McIntyre, who ran picture houses and vaudeville theaters, hired him to lead audiences at her People's Palace in sing-alongs where, between movies, the words to current hits were flashed on the screen. He graduated to trap drums and sound effects, becoming adept at not only providing rat-tat-tat gunshots for the westerns, but also the moos of cows and snorts of horses. He later incorporated these vocal effects into hits of the day, inspired by the scatty singing of self-styled "Ragtime King" Gene Greene, whose records were riddled with snatches of pig latin followed by volleys of pure blather, but very musical and very exciting. Greene's "King of the Bungaloos" had Cliff in fits, and the younger fellow soon had the madness corralled and part of his act.

Miss Lily let Cliff perform in her vaudeville theatres for a while, but pretty soon he was again on the road—on the circuits and then off again for odd jobs like driving a grocery wagon in San Antonio and demonstrating "nasal humantones" ("eefing"?) in the basement of Bailey's department store in Cleveland. In the 1930s, when he was a star, he told Wally Kingsland of *Popular Songs* magazine about the humantones, adding: "At Bailey's I met Charles 'Flatiron' Worth, a well-known clown, acting as Santa Claus. He was a real friend. When he accepted an offer to join the Reserve Photoplay Company, he also got me a job as comedian. Well, that company folded and I caught on again to peddling magazines, working my way through the college of life!"

Eventually Cliff Edwards reached the big and bustling showbiz center of Chicago around 1917. The timing was right. The uke was busting out all over. So was jazz, the craze that would soon put both ragtime and Hawaii in the shade . . .

In the Windy City there was a promising music scene led in print by Will Rossiter's publishing house, busy printing old rag songs like "Some of These Days" and new hits like "The Darktown Strutters' Ball." Stuttering Joe Frisco, an eccentric dancer known for syncopated slides and shuffles synchronized with a fast-shooting cigar and a derby he cleverly caught while it was trying to escape in flight, took "Darktown" as his theme song. He was

at present strutting his stuff at Big Jim Colosimo's restaurant, a swell spot noted for its well-bodied dancing girls and large dance band. Big Jim ran Chicago's gangster underworld and recognized the potent mix of strong dance music, strong drink, and strapping girls. He liked to fiddle with the band arrangements.

Frisco made Big Jim laugh at his claim that he was a direct descendant of Austrian Emperor Franz Joseph, of the family who'd started the current war in Europe, and Jim guffawed when, at a benefit performance where Frisco was to follow visiting star Enrico Caruso, the hoofer leaned over to the hallowed tenor and ordered, "Don't sing 'Darktown Strutters' Ball'—I use it as my big finish."

Joe had taught the tune to the boys from New Orleans who were presently in the big time over in New York, appearing as the Original Dixieland Jazz Band and, reputedly, selling millions of records. He was proud of this because he'd first spotted the boys' talent in New Orleans when a bunch of them backed his act at the Young Men's Gymnastic. He brought them up to Chicago to do the same for his act at the Lamb's Club. That was in 1914, and now in 1917 their jazz music was making history. And he, the great Frisco, was still hoofing in Chicago clubs and dives, at the mercy of hoodlums, protected for the time being by Big Jim.

Joe was looking for a way out and up—for someone to spice up his act with some hot music and a new angle. He was past the stage where, in order to pay the rent, he'd sneak his landlady's print of "The Last Supper" to a pawnshop and offer it up for twenty-five cents a head.

At this point Cliff Edwards, new in town, was working tables at a chain called Thompson's One-Arm Restaurants. Since there was no pianist or band, he couldn't perform properly. But . . .

One night in his digs, he noticed his landlady's mandolin hanging over the fireplace (landladies were crucial factors in showbiz life back then). He removed four strings and started fooling with it, trying to play a tune. A few weeks later he was strumming acceptably. The landlady encouraged him, the restaurant customers clapped for him. He thought he'd better go out and buy a proper ukulele. There were plenty for sale, both in stores and hockshops. He picked out a used Martin. Nobody taught him, no method book was consulted. "I don't understand my technique even now," he confessed two decades and several fortunes later.

He graduated from the One-Arm joint to the Arsonia Cafe on the strength of his novel singing with the guttural noises and uke strumming. The uke allowed him to be mobile, moving from table to table, garnering tips in his hat, answering requests ranging from "I'm Sorry I Made You Cry" to "Bing! Bang! Bing 'Em on the Rhine." The war was on, but he got a deferment as a "theatrical entertainer." Bob Carleton, the new café pianist, wasn't so lucky, but he was proud of having served in the Navy even if there wasn't any action. Bob came back with a catchy thing he'd made up—one of those hey-nonny-no tunes you can't get off your mind and whose lyrics are child's play—"Ja-Da (Ja-Da, Ja-Da, Jing, Jing, Jing)"—yet "soothing and appealing," as the singer points out. Perfect for a war-weary world, fed up with noble causes like making the world safe for democracy. Like jazz, an antidote for the real blues.

Carleton and Edwards did so well with the song that they got a booking in vaudeville, a proper one. And Edwards now had a nickname that would later be his stage name: Spot, a tiresome beer-slinger at the Arsonia, could never remember Cliff's name so took to shouting "Hey, you—Ukulele Ike—come and pick up the Pabsts!"

When the pair completed the loop and were back in Chicago, Carleton decided to concentrate on his songwriting, since "Ja-Da" was selling like crazy and all the jazz bands were recording it. As luck would have it, and it often does, Edwards's act had been caught by Joe Frisco, who now, due to his self-coronation as King of Jazz Dance, was cashing in on the new craze. Frisco had been offered a slot at the nation's top vaude house, the Palace in New York, provided he had a self-sustaining act. This Ike with his songs and his uke and the oddball drumming with all the animal noises, plus a pretty girl to even things out, seemed just the ticket. "The Boy with the Ukulele" they called him in vaudeville—"Ukulele Ike" was still a nickname.

Edwards took a pay cut to play the Palace with Frisco. They did their act in the autumn of 1918 when everyone was in a jolly mood because the war was over. A brief spot in that year's edition of the *Ziegfeld Follies* showed Edwards he was part of the Big Time. He was on his way, but there'd be ups and downs, and he still relied on a partner. After Frisco went his own way, Cliff teamed up with one Pierce Keegan, another dancer, and they were billed topically as "Jazz as Is." They hit the Palace in 1920, and by this time Edwards was advertised as "Ukulele Ike." Next we find him in blackface partnering Lou Clayton, a Brooklyn-born (as Louis Finkelstein) soft-shoe stepper with a poker face and a nose for business. (Clayton later partnered with Jimmy Durante and Eddie Jackson in a famously frenetic nightclub act; offstage he became Durante's manager.)

The original World War I sheet music.
From the collection of Flea Market Music.

What these various configurations did in their act (apart from wearing boot polish) I don't know—probably a mishmash of anything goes, as most of vaudeville tended to be. Only the star acts shone with a hard, bright, and arrow-sharp personality.

It was later as a "single" that Edwards got his best reviews: in November 1921, "Conn" in *The Dramatic Mirror* wrote about how, again in blackface, the boy with the "restless ukulele" and a special way with the old "St. Louis Blues," had "all the glorious jazz possible and went over with a bang . . . His voice imitation of a clarinet is clever and he uses it in every number. Maybe it's personality, but anyway we didn't have half enough of Edwards and when he jazzes we just can't make our feet behave."

Cliff was being handled by Max Hart, the manager who'd taken over the Original Dixieland Jazz Band on the advice of Al Jolson (via Joe Frisco), and had pushed the Southern boys into the spotlight. Hart now secured Edwards a part in Mae West's *The Mimic World*, his first Broadway appearance. Unfortunately, the twenty-five-scene revue—really no more than a series of vaudeville acts with West demonstrating her shimmy dance and doing impersonations, including one of the star Nazimova ("Jazzimova")—was a flop and closed within the month. "The very peak of worthlessness," said *The Billboard*. Edwards wasn't mentioned.

He got his big break in 1924 with *Lady, Be Good!*, the first true musical of the Jazz Age, with the hot songs of George and Ira Gershwin sending a shudder down the stiff European back of operetta, the hoary old form then cluttering up Broadway. Edwards, now recognized as "Ukulele Ike," had no integrated role in the play—he just strolled onstage in the middle of

From the collection of Flea Market Music.

an argument between the boy and girl and proceeded to render "Fascinating Rhythm" with only his ukulele to aid him. He stopped the show, he and his "lamb chop."

Now the number is a tricky one precisely because of its fascinating or eccentric rhythm, the jerky dives when the words hit in places you don't expect. Weak beats—devilish clever. Not the natural syncopation of the classic ragtime but now seen as the last word, the bee's knees in modernity, by the jaded sophisticates of first night Broadway. The jerkiness woke them up. Edwards was masterful in the tricksy bits, casually singing as if the song were all his own work, with his uke running along in tandem. Fred and Adele Astaire danced along too. Fred had seen Edwards and Frisco at the Palace and wanted to learn from both of them. He could certainly learn from Edwards's recording of "Fascinating

Ukulele Ike's showstopper
from *Sunny*.
From the collection of Flea Market Music.

"Paddlin' Madelin' Home" and in the *Ziegfeld Follies of 1927* with Eddie Cantor and Ruth Etting. He was moving with the stars. The next stop was the movies, where he was to remain for a decade or so.

Irving Thalberg, boy wonder producer at MGM, caught Ukulele Ike in his vaudeville act at the Or-

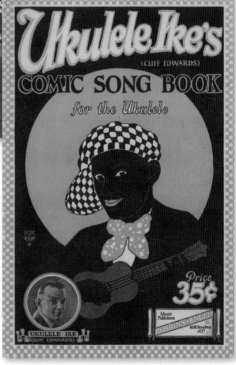

Rhythm," which, when released on the Pathé label, became a hit.

Musicians from George Gershwin to top jazzmen were impressed by Edwards's musicianship. He was the first to admit he couldn't read the black ink and had to get a pianist to demonstrate a new number. But he was proud of his three-octave range and that he could sing in any key—even those yet to be invented. "Some loud and some soft." Here was a character, good copy for the press boys. Always on, always merry.

Now a certified showstopper, he went on to do his specialty act in Jerome Kern and Oscar Hammerstein II's *Sunny*, where he sang

**Ukulele Ike depicted in blackface
as he was in his 1920s act.**
From the collection of Flea Market Music.

pheum Theatre in Los Angeles and signed him for the company's *All Star Musical Extravaganza*. A parade of the studio's contract artists, the huge part-color folly was ultimately titled *The Hollywood Revue of 1929*. Hollywood, tottering in terror at the first breaths of the talkies, had bought Tin Pan Alley, and every studio was filling its films with song and dance because, on the strength of Al Jolson's *The Jazz Singer*, that's what seemed to sell.

Ike has two numbers in the picture, both goodies. First, in a rain slicker and hat, he solos "Singin' in the Rain," fingers flicking over the strings to produce a complete and satisfying sound. No need for an orchestra. The chorus is dead simple, but the verse is quite difficult: it keeps changing keys. He breezes through it, though. Then the girls and boys take over for some dancing. Ike comes back with a full chorus of scatting.

In his second number, he has a chance to be a sweet balladeer with "Nobody But You," an old-fashioned charmer by veteran songwriter Gus ("By the Light of the Silvery Moon") Edwards. That Ike's costumed as a minstrel man doesn't take away from the poignancy of the song. He proves there's more to Ukulele Ike's vocals than "eefin'."

MGM had high hopes for Ike. In the movie's press campaign, there was a tale about a besotted Minneapolis housewife so in love with his records that she played them night and day, thus causing her husband to seek a divorce. At his new home in Hollywood, he was hounded by fans who not only wanted an autograph, but also his instruments, or so the studio publicists claimed: "A ukulele sees pretty hard service in his hands and doesn't last long. He is besieged by souvenir hunters who gain admittance to the studio and invariably ask him for one of his old ukuleles."

As early as October 1930, he was telling the celebrity columnists he wanted to get rid of his ukes. "He is determined," wrote one, "to be a full-fledged actor and not merely a song and dance man . . . He is determined to make the name 'Ukulele Ike' only a memory."

This was not to be. He had to keep working in the whimsical persona he had created. During the 1930s and into the '50s he played supporting roles in dozens of movies, especially westerns. He also played an uncredited bellhop, a hog caller, an undertaker, and the off-screen voice of a "reminiscing soldier" in *Gone with the Wind*.

He swapped uke tunes with his fellow MGM contract player Buster Keaton (no slouch on the lamb chop himself). He told a fanciful story of his life in *Take a Chance* (1933) in "I Did It with My Ukulele," a pungent piece of special material written for him by ace Broadway songwriters Jay Gorney and Yip Harburg.

"You gotta romance 'em," he tells lovelorn James Dunn in reference to the uses of the uke as they sit on the bed in their undershirts. "Get 'em out in the moonlight." He goes on to wonder rhetorically, in the verse of the song, how he ever got by when "things were not so hot." Well, it's simple: his little pal "protected me from every care and strife." And what's more: "I never took a lesson in my life."

Off goes the movie into his story of being shipwrecked on a tropical isle populated by non-vegetarians, but how he charmed these Polynesians with his uke music so that soon they were hula dancing sexily around him. Why, a saucy "South Sea mama really shakes a mean pajama." Eventually he leaves this

Hawaiʻi-like paradise to return to civilization. Left behind is a string of wives and children. As he tells Dunn, the uke "got me in and out of plenty of jams."

Edwards was already in quite a few jams himself. His private life was shambolic, had been for years, and was made public in the papers.

"Uke Ike Humble as Wife Fixes Price of Pride," cried the *Los Angeles Times* on August 23, 1930:

"Don't call me 'mister' and don't call me Clif-ford, I'm just plain Ukulele Ike, and although my voice goes into the best homes, on the radio, I've got no social standing whatever." Thus did Cliff Edwards, songwriter and actor, dispose of his wife's plea that she had to have $250 a week alimony to maintain her social position as Mrs. Irene Edwards.

Ike offered to sing her a couple of songs as alimony.

Mrs. Edwards replied, sotto voce, that she had listened to her husband's songs long enough.

Ike then testified he was broke. Mrs. Edwards got no alimony, but she did get one third of his future earnings.

Next year he got his chance for divorce after he and a bunch of private detectives raided his Santa Monica beach house and surprised Irene and Austin "Skin" Young, a notorious phi-landerer and dance band musician, in an after-sex situation. The judge granted the divorce on the grounds of "extreme mental cruelty."

A little later, his first wife, Mrs. Gertrude Ryrholm, who'd made a few thousand back in their 1923 divorce, popped up to demand ex-tra child support: their twelve-year-old son had just had both legs amputated due to a Chicago freight train accident. Ike was ordered to pay up. No sooner had he done that than Irene re-turned to court to demand almost $25,000 as her chunk of Ike's MGM salary. Lawyers were hounding him for unpaid fees, too.

So he flew off to Las Vegas and married Nancy Dover, a kid actress. Right after the wedding he was sued for unpaid bills. There fol-lowed demands for unpaid child support. And on and on . . .

In 1933 he filed for bankruptcy: he owed $68,000; he owned $200 in clothes. No men-tion of ukes. Wife Nancy was being sued for back rent owed on their Beverly Hills home. Ike made up for his debts in movie and stage and radio work. In 1935 he was discharged from bankruptcy. In 1936 Nancy was grant-ed a divorce. She claimed he was out of this world. "You mean profligate?" said the judge. "I mean—he would sign anything," said Nancy. "After I'd beg him not to get into any more law-suits, he'd go out and sign contracts with two or three managers at a time and naturally they would all sue later."

Gambling, drinking, and battles with the taxman didn't help matters. Then in 1939, he established a link with Walt Disney that was to aid him the rest of his life. In 1939, after thirty-six actor/singers had auditioned before him for the voice of Jiminy Cricket in *Pinocchio*, a feature-length cartoon, in walked Ike and Uncle Walt picked him, loved him.

Edwards endeared himself to the cast for his kindness—in the studio he sat next to the boy voicing Pinocchio rather than in his as-signed high stool. Between takes he pulled out a uke and did a few funny numbers, grinning and eye-popping in a hat with the brim pushed back. His recording voice, his vaudeville timing and sheer professionalism, pleased the animators.

However, there was to be no ukulele and no scatting, no Ukulele Ikeing in the picture.

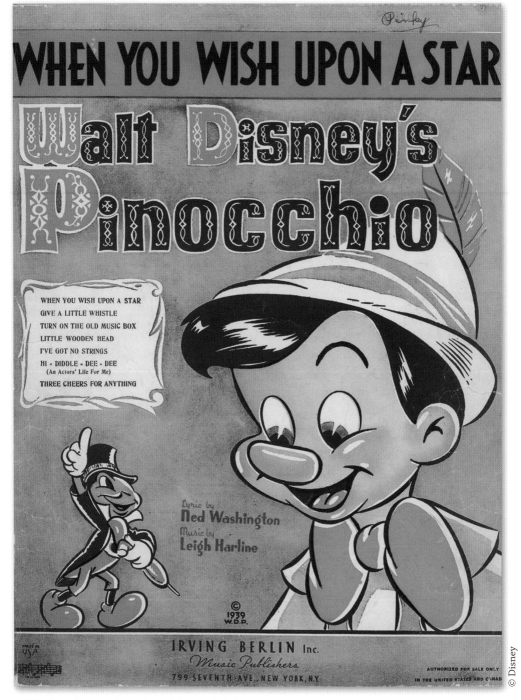

Cliff Edwards was the voice of Jiminy Cricket in Walt Disney's *Pinocchio*.

From the collection of Flea Market Music.

Instead Edwards played quirky sober, putting in a moving, even thrilling vocal on "When You Wish Upon a Star," which floats ethereally over the opening credits. His was the voice of an ideal childhood spent, perhaps, in Hannibal. Or any place in your best memories—truly a sound for all time. The song, by Ned Washington and Leigh Harline, published by Irving Berlin, won an Academy Award in 1940. Edwards got a flat fee.

It wasn't enough to help him in a court case that year. This time it concerned his hair, or lack of it. Miss Georgia George, beautician, claimed she had made "beautiful and healthy hair" to sprout on Edwards's bald head—"As barren as a ukulele," she said. He agreed that hair had appeared but said it was "not nice," and he refused to pay the $324 bill.

Next year, in March 1941, he was declared bankrupt again, with debts of $26,000 and assets listed as "clothing, household goods and ornaments= $150; radio and recording phonograph= $300; two ukuleles= $10." The *Los Angeles Times* wrote: "He still has his ukuleles but jobs have been few and far between. He can still sing and dance, but opportunity has been lacking." Chimed in Edwards: "But I'll make a comeback, you'll see!"

This was never to happen as big as the old days. He was reduced to playing Charley Foy's Supper Club in the San Fernando Valley by night after sidekicking in B westerns by day. He had a fifteen-minute television show of "songs and chatter" for CBS in 1949, but that year, while living splendidly at the Waldorf-Astoria in New York, he yet again declared bankruptcy.

Walt Disney stayed true. As a regular on *The Mickey Mouse Club*, Ike was introduced to a whole audience of children who adored his avuncular impishness. The Mouseketeers were

appreciative, but from a distance: the little old man exuded "brandy breath" in all directions. Off the set, he gave free shows at hospitals, where patients recognized the voice of Jiminy Cricket. At other shows, though, there was whispering among the organizers about his drunkenness.

In 1965 he voiced his last picture, an animated western. In 1969, as a penniless Medi-Cal patient he moved to the Virgil Convalescent Hospital in Hollywood. Walt Disney Productions, which had adopted his recording of "When You Wish Upon a Star" as their corporate anthem, paid for his upkeep. Nobody at the nursing home had any idea who he'd been; nobody came to see him. He died there of heart failure on July 17, 1971.

For four days his body lay unclaimed at the Los Angeles County Hospital, until the administrator's office worked out who he was and what he'd been. Somehow the news director of KHMO radio in Hannibal, Missouri, put two and two together and told his listeners. Their chamber of commerce arranged for internment services. The Disney people got wind of what was happening or not happening. They fixed up and financed the funeral service and burial at Valhalla Memorial Park, near the Burbank airport. Oliver Hardy, another ukulele player, is buried close to Ike.

Aside from the mess of his personal life, which mainly had to do with women and money, Edwards seems to have been a Falstaffian figure, always good company, a man's man to be convivial with whether it be at watering hole, racetrack, or gambling den. Everybody knew him, from the postmaster-general to Clark Gable, and clapped when he arrived at a niterie because they knew that now, with the life of the party present, the fun would begin.

Generous to a fault, he invited struggling musicians to live at his Hollywood apartment when he was between marriages. He threw parties for his pals (and anybody else who happened to be around) aboard his government surplus boat as it chugged through the looking glass. Sometimes there were aftermaths to the good times, as when he was arrested in Glendale in the late 1950s for "dodging imaginary objects" while riding a motorcycle.

This front of eternal merriment coupled with a sincerely sentimental side is conveyed on his hundreds of recordings. They are his legacy and through them he will live forever.

The early acoustic recordings from 1922, with jazzy outfits like Bailey's Lucky Seven and Ladd's Black Aces, are shot through with scatting and capture the very essence of the frenetic aspect of the Jazz Age. All he does in "Homesick" is contribute "vocal effects," but it's enough to electrify a tinny acoustic. In 1924, when he was in *Lady, Be Good!* on Broadway, he cut the title number with only his uke, but the effect is that of a one-man band complete in itself. His forcefully staggered vocal triplets get the lyrics across with emphatic meaning, which is more than can be said for later versions by respected jazz singers with little interest in words and too much pride in pyrotechnic chops.

The same can be said of "Fascinating Rhythm." Ira Gershwin's throwaway words are given special accents and attention. The result is definitive—Fred Astaire imitates Ike in his recorded version. We know that Astaire worshipped him. We also know that around that time Bing Crosby and the Rhythm Boys listened with enthusiastic carefulness to the exciting interpretations Ike made of songs that were later to become jazz standards. On "Dinah," backed by his Hot Combination, Ike has a splendid exchange of licks with Red Nichols. On "Sunday," as the jazzers toot, he relaxes, stretching out on the bars and making the song sound like he's making it up as he's moving along. Like a fellow telling you a story from a bar stool.

Edwards comes close to his own sad story in "Anything You Say," a 1928 electrical recording written by hit maker Walter Donaldson. The lady lover is described as one who must be obeyed, must always have her own way, even if it's a demand for a Cadillac coupe. Edwards was between marriages at the time; Donaldson, although officially married, liked to travel with a "nurse."

Dominating all these discs, like a great conductor, is the constantly driving force of the Ike uke, a harmonic drum. He might strike percussively hard but he could also finger sweet—as is shown on the beautiful and yearning "I'll See You in My Dreams." And he's heartbreaking on "I'm Losing You." The subtle arrangement has the band laying out in the verse and first chorus as voice and uke, with a regretful celesta behind, describe a rather disturbing situation: "Although we pet, I understand what love I get is secondhand."

Similarly he's crooner-quiet and thoughtful on the philosophical "It's Only a Paper Moon"—life as just "a melody played in a penny arcade"—recorded in October 1933 when he was in bankruptcy. Guitarist Dick McDonough provides sterling accompaniment with Edwards joining him near the end. A satisfying mix, guitar and uke—a perfect blend.

The day before he'd cut a bunch of risqué party songs for limited and special consumption: his composition "I'm Going to Give It to Mary with Love" is rife with double meanings—she'll "take it right in her hand" and stroke it. Of course, all's well when he reveals the thing in question is merely a kitten, a necklace, a diamond. Edwards needed the money. Anything for a job.

That was the case in 1956, when he hadn't made a commercial recording in ages. Disneyland Records, with Uncle Walt's blessing, gave him a day at Capitol's superb new tower studio to do as he pleased with old warhorse numbers. Backing him was the Wonderland Jazz Band, led by Disney staff composer George Bruns on tuba and trombone. George Probert, a Disney music editor and assistant director, was on clarinet. Ike had recorded with such Dixieland revivalist bands as Bob Scobey's Frisco Jazz Band and the Firehouse Five Plus Two.

Now George Probert has played with me too over the years. When I asked him for his memories of that session, he opened up like a sunny sky after a storm.

"It was the happiest recording date I ever had!" So what was Ike like in person? What did he talk about? "He never uttered a word. He just sang and strummed and then put on his hat with the turned-up brim and left the building."

George had seen Edwards around the studios, where Walt kept him on payroll as Jiminy Cricket. He used to sit alone on a bench in the sun with his hat pushed back and his cheeks blown out and a funny sort of fixed smile. Never spoke to anybody.

In the studio he was put in an isolation booth, alone with his uke. The band couldn't hear him but he could hear them okay. The ar-

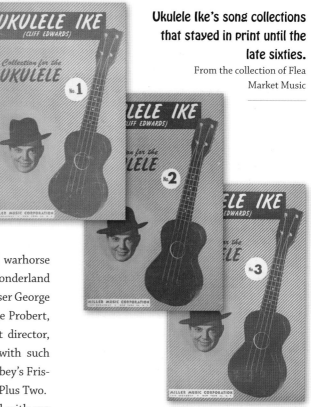

Ukulele Ike's song collections that stayed in print until the late sixties.

From the collection of Flea Market Music

rangements were created on the spot, suggested by his pianist, Marvin Ash, who'd accompanied him on an Australian tour sometime back. Among the old reliables were "Singin' in the Rain" and "Ja Da" (which despite his having helped become a hit he'd never before recorded). Sixteen tracks were cut that day, every one in a single take. When Edwards sang he was animated as hell, happy as a lark; between takes he was sober as a judge. George, who'd had experience of this kind of behavior, reckoned Edwards was a "reverse personality": bubbly when drunk, dead flat when sober.

They assembled in the control room for the playbacks. The bandsmen were amazed. Thanks to Capitol's full-range microphones and sympathetic room sound, Edward's voice was

SINGIN' IN THE RAIN
I'LL SEE YOU IN MY DREAMS
I'M SORRY I MADE YOU CRY
K-K-K-KATY
WHEN YOU WORE A TULIP
SLEEPY TIME GAL
AT SUNDOWN
I CRIED FOR YOU
JA DA
JUNE NIGHT
SUNDAY
THE DARKTOWN STRUTTERS' BALL
SWINGIN' DOWN THE LANE
TOOT TOOT TOOTSIE
NO NO NORA
FIVE FEET TWO, EYES OF BLUE

© Disney

From the collection of Flea Market Music.

captured as never before: richer and fruitier and deeper than when he was being Jiminy Cricket at Disney. Coming through the speakers was a guy with fantastic jazz chops. "Singin' in the Rain" sounded far hipper than Gene Kelly in the movie. The uke playing was right in the groove, and the scatting was up there with Satchmo and Ella.

George and the boys had never heard the Ukulele Ike of his Jazz Age heyday. He was just a Mr. Cricket to them. When the LP, *Ukulele Ike Sings Again*, was released, George went up to Edwards as he sat on his bench sunning and asked him to sign it. Ike wrote "Jiminy Cricket" on the cover.

Two decades later, at Dr. Demento's house in Pasadena, I was exposed to "June Night" from that same LP. The stark but original combination of Ike, uke, and a tuba was a revelation to me. That art can be so stripped-down simple—no monster orchestra, no forest-thick arrangement, no arm-waving conductor—was a lesson for life in general. Thank you, Ike, for your message of salvation in the true essence of things!

MORE HEROES
AND ONE HEROINE
FRANK CRUMIT

Frank Crumit actually precedes Cliff Edwards, but doesn't have the kudos—despite selling a lot of records, especially in Britain and its Empire, and becoming a 1930s radio star in company with his wife.

He was a uke-playing pro in vaudeville and on Broadway, years before Ike. He's older than all the other "Heroes" and seems to have been strumming even before the Hawaiian Invasion. He was the first mainlander to make commercial recordings. He's also the only Hero from our Golden Age who graduated from college.

Pleasantly beefsteak-faced and with the demeanor of a non-caning schoolmaster, Crumit came from a classy background. But despite lacking street credibility, he was a skilled ukester with an un-edgy folksy mass appeal in his genial and stylish manner.

It was a manner very different from the Hawaiians of "The Bird of Paradise." They had an erotic exoticism; he had a restful elegance, promising a few good stories on the golf links prior to cocktails in the club.

He was born in 1889 in Jackson, Ohio, to a blue-blooded County family. His grandfather, known as The Grey Eagle due to an imperious mien, had been a surgeon in the Civil War, wielding saw and whiskey bottle with a certainty that won him plaudits from both hospital staff and patients. Frank Crumit Sr., the son, became a banker—and widower, leaving Frank Jr. to be raised by his Aunt Patsy.

She knew the old Southern folk tales and songs so well and delivered them with such an authentic "darky" drawl that their black cook pronounced her "scandalous funny." Auntie's ward watched and digested, taking her loamy folklore to the academies and colleges he attended. At the first university, he pretended to study medicine; at the second one he took up electrical engineering and managed to get invited to join the exclusive Phi Delta Theta fraternity. It's amazing he graduated with honors, because his studies had to share time with stardom on the baseball and football fields—he wrote Ohio State's "Buckeye Battle Cry" marching song—as well as nighttime leadership of the glee and mandolin clubs, where he caused laughter with folksy songs like "Abdul Abulbul Amir," "Riding Down to Bangor," and the minstrel songs of Stephen Foster.

Mostly he accompanied his warm and friendly voice, a natural light tenor, with a guitar and banjo. However, he got a lot more attention when he started to strum a ukulele. This was around 1912 and there were precious few of the cute little music boxes in the country. One of his professors suggested the ukulele be placed on the curriculum and that Crumit be made teacher.

But Frank had other plans. First, encouraged by the college crowd, he substituted for a local vaudeville act that failed to show up. He did well and next he was on the circuits as The One Man Glee Club, a simple act in which he strolled up to the footlight with a chair, sat down, pulled out his uke, and drawled a few mildly humorous and certainly inoffensive ditties of his own making, such as "The Prune Song" and "A Parlor Is a Pleasant Place to Sit in Sunday Night." A little progress around the country and he was being billed as "A Comedian Who Can Sing, Play Instruments and Tell a Story."

Somehow or other, he drifted over to 1913 London where, we are told, he put over the latest syncopated songs in revues and music halls as an ad hoc member of the American Ragtime

Invasion team, which, led by Irving Berlin, had had the British in their thrall for a few years. He liked England and lingered awhile, testing the trout fishing of the south and the gorse links of Scotland. He returned via Liverpool on the *SS Celtic*, in time to miss the great European war, which would have rather spoiled things. In 1915, he's in New York. *Variety* reports that Frank Crumit is the "sole male member" of a restaurant revue called *Keep Moving* where there's no cover charge, because the cabaret scene is wilting and anything to get the customers in. We hope his family and college pals weren't aware of this down-market development—for a college man from a decent family.

New York turned out to be good for him: in 1919, he was cast as the leading man in a Broadway musical comedy billed as "Smart Comedy with Smart Music," but the songs weren't his—yet. Two years later he starred in *Tangerine* with Julia Sanderson, a seasoned Broadway beauty (she'd introduced Jerome Kern's first big hit, "They Didn't Believe Me" onstage in 1914), and now she sang Crumit's catchy but chromatic song "Sweet Lady," which he'd written with a fellow sporting the odd name of Zoob. Julia and Frank hit it off, and the public liked the magical chemistry of the duo too. They played together in several Broadway musicals including *Oh, Kay!*, a Gershwin show, until they got married in 1927 and settled down in Massachusetts in a spot they named "Dunrovin" because they were done with roving.

Instead they chose to be unhurried and stationary in radio, eventually becoming household names as the "Singing Sweethearts of the Air," even as the air below became harsh and sour with the Great Depression. Radio thrived above the clangor as the couple made the journey from home to the New York studio for their daytime variety show and their evening quiz show, *Battle of the Sexes*. It was all very comfortable and comforting. There was plenty of time for golf and bridge and jokes with the country club members. Frank was such a personable chap, so beloved by his fellow performers, that he was easily elected president of the Lambs Club in 1935.

To be a Lamb was to be in an exclusive band of show business folk who were also gentlemen or wanted to be. Irving Berlin and George M.Cohan were members, and when Fred Astaire was elected he likened it to being knighted. Of course, Frank Crumit never took his uke to the club. I mention the above because Cliff Edwards would never have been considered. Nor, I believe, would any other of our heroes.

The couple had just started two new radio series in 1943 when Frank died of a heart attack that September. It put an abrupt end to a contented marriage and a satisfying business setup, as well as a career that's been a relaxing pleasure to describe. Widow Julia withdrew from the public eye and ear and was never heard about again until her obituaries in 1969.

Frank Crumit was the first of our heroes to record. From 1919 onwards and into the 1930s he was extremely prolific, releasing over 250 records in genres ranging from Tin Pan Alley ("My Little Bimbo Down on the Bamboo Isle") and Broadway ("Mountain Greenery") to black folk songs ("Down in de Cane Brake") and a comical tragedy from Dublin ("Abdul Abulbul Amir"). He dealt with horse racing, bootlegging, insurance, the Wall Street crash, and, naturally, golf. He never tackled any hot lovemaking.

The acoustic recordings are hard to appreciate—the horn makes his voice metallic and nasal and, as the Hawaiian bands were to dis-

Crumit ran the gamut from sophisticated Broadway material to down-homey melodies.
From the collection of Harold Jacobs.

From the collection of Flea Market Music.

cover, a solo ukulele doesn't come across as well as massed ukes striking hard like an advancing army. With electrical recording, Crumit's voice is opened up with all its fullness and intrinsic benevolence—still with a slightness that is confidential and trustworthy, breathing brandy, but not too much, and only in a social way.

A good example is "Abdul Abulbul Amir," the original of which had been written as a "seven-canto drama" in 1877 for a smoking concert in Trinity College Dublin (my old alma mater) by Percy French, banjo entertainer and undergraduate. French failed to copyright it, and pirated copies got to America, where Crumit developed his own version at Ohio State. Abdul and the Russian Count Ivan Skivinsky Skivar still knife each other to death, but there are far fewer funny names than in the original. However, there were enough to amuse the polite public, those who didn't care for dirty blues or jazz babies. Crumit's record sold well enough to warrant sequels involving Abdul's return from the grave, followed by a grandson.

His ukulele is heard favorably on "Ukulele Lady," a hit by mainlanders Gus Kahn and Richard Whiting, full of wicki wacki woos and thus far removed from the real thing in Honolulu. The combination of uke and guitar and nothing else is a winning blend and, to my mind, more satisfying than solo uke. All that's needed is a bass and it would be perfect.

Crumit was at his best with small units and in the 1930s when he moved to Decca, then controlled by the British, his group was very sympa-

thetic to his suave voice and sly and wry quiet humor. He was smooth at singing about violent death without giving offense—as in the Abdul numbers, as well as his cleaned-up "Frankie and Johnny"—and on Decca he delivered a hillbilly death-ballad spoof called "The Old Apple Tree," which has a father lynched by his neighbors for taking a widow away on a jamboree.

Crumit's 1930s records never did well in America, but in Britain he was much in demand. Respectable people who weren't too keen on hot jazz relished the gentle Crumit style. Amongst them was a prep-school master and ex-sea captain who made these records available to me when I was eight and one of his pupils.

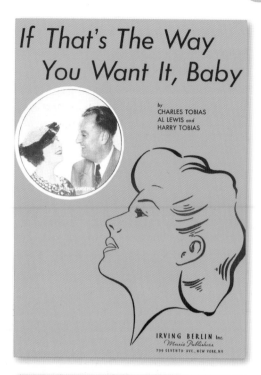

A most unlikely offering from such a suave clubman!

From the collection of Harold Jacobs.

How I loved setting the tone arm on the electric radiogram with its glowing city of vacuum tubes that seemed like New York at night, and settling down on the carpet in the master's tobacco-flavored hut! How happy I was to be transported to a wild and woolly America made palatable by tubby-sounding Mr. "Croomit," as I called him, an uncle-figure who, in my dreams, might well be coming to teach geography and games next term!

WENDELL HALL

Rootin', tootin' Wendell Hall, the self-promoting "Red-Headed Music Maker" from Kansas, with the attention-commanding voice, clever habit of clipping his Gs, and million-selling record of his very own, "It Ain't Gonna Rain No Mo'," is a very different kettle of fish from clubman Crumit with his plus-four knickers, fraternity pin, and store of genteel folk songs.

The ukulele, of which Hall had examples in different sizes and timbres and which he thrashed (and never thrummed) with a rough vigor, is not usually associated with the birth of country music. However, what we have here is a proud man standing tall at the start of that industry, long before it got its respectable name of "country and western." Wendell Hall was producing for the early 1920s "hill-billy" market and, as a founder, was well aware of his part in it.

Working with fellow Kansan Carson Robison, a guitarist and whistler, Hall was happy to, as his partner later explained it, "give the

A venerable comic song rendered anew by Crumit.

From the collection of Harold Jacobs.

natives exactly what they wanted, which, naturally enough, was something they knew . . . "

He didn't latch onto the uke and its brothers until 1922. Initially Hall had been appearing in vaudeville as a singing xylophonist and finding himself out of work. In Chicago he got a job song-plugging for Forster, a big local music publisher trying to compete with New York's Tin Pan Alley. They needed a new angle, a niche market, and they found it thanks to the bustling and booming new industry of commercial radio. The Chicago stations, owned by companies like Sears, Roebuck and Co. (WLS—World's Largest Store), beamed all over the Midwest and were gratefully received by the rural community. Entertainers were few and far between, and so anything that tickled their particular funny bone or plucked at their heartstrings was welcomed and blessed and was the subject of fan letters to the radio bosses. The music they craved might sell flour, oil lamps, or long johns—anything and everything!

Wendell Hall, in order to be more mobile in his song-plugging travels round the hinterlands, had abandoned the xylophone as too cumbersome and taken up the ukulele. The farmers and their wives adored the homespun songs of mountain, range, and plain he offered after he'd finished plugging the standard love ballads and jazz tunes. Back in Chicago, he got time on KYW as a singing comedian ("A Whole Show in Himself")—the stations were hungry for music filler between the ads for seed or farm implements—and he was an instant hit with old-time numbers about church, home, mother, and how much better things were in the good old days.

At the end of 1923, on his travels again, he wandered into Gennett Records, a branch of the Starr Piano Company, in Richmond, Indiana. He was hoping to cut a few sides whenever the passing trains permitted. A pretty crude operation (lots of hiss and crackle in the finished product), Gennett was known for its black blues and jazz and its white gospel.

There happened to be a convention of piano dealers going on in the factory and the boys were tucking in to a slap-up buffet luncheon. Hall, his hair mussed up and wearing clothes that resembled a tramp's outfit, joined the line

Wendell Hall's million-selling self-written "folk" song.
From the collection of Flea Market Music.

Wendell Hall's Ukulele Method—note that it was edited by May Singhi Breen.
From the collection of Flea Market Music.

and then as payment, pulled out his uke and entertained the dealers with a selection of his "old-time Southern songs." They found him hellaciously funny and quaint, and the Gennett boss noticed the reaction and invited him to record a couple: "The Red Headed Music Maker" and "It Ain't Gonna Rain No Mo'."

Now "Rain" was the comic song Hall had gotten the most requests for on radio and Forster had agreed to publish, so he knew that even if the record guys screwed him he stood to make money as the songwriter. Who knows where he'd found the song—some of the piano dealers swore they'd heard saltier versions by "colored" men down in Dixie turpentine camps;

others said they'd danced all their lives to this jig tune in the Blue Ridge Mountains of Virginia and among Carolina pines.

Hall's concoction is a two-chord novelty with a can't-get-out-of-the-head melody and stubby short verses telling, like crazed minstrelsy from the cabbage patch, wise old saws and recounting misadventures with bedbugs and bullfrogs, mosquitoes and wildcats, as well as about an unfortunate man who expires near a sewer. Ultra-simple—just Hall, in baritone and falsetto with a little bit of scatting, accompanied by his thrashed ukulele.

Gennett wished him luck and let him have—at his request—a test pressing. On he traveled to New York, where he played the pressing for Victor Records, a major organization. They loved it and contracted Hall to make a new version with their superior equipment. The result, although the same routine as on the Gennett, was much livelier, spotted with gurgling laughter and bursting with personality. Victor promised to get behind it. Hall promised to plug it. He embarked on a national tour of radio stations. Victor was thrilled. Forster was thrilled.

The country embraced his song as theirs, even the city slickers, and soon folks added their own verses ("How in the heck can I wash my neck / If it ain't gonna rain no more?") to a tune that was vaguely familiar. Within a year, record and sheet music had sold over a million copies each and Forster was offering a special version with twenty-four new verses. They were also getting into the virgin business of marketing a new kind of old-timey music to appeal to their goldmine rural audience.

Meanwhile Wendell Hall, now the first true radio star, was exploiting his rural image like there was no tomorrow. And, of course,

Headstock of the Wendell Hall Red Head Ukulele.
From the collection of Flea Market Music.

in the world of pop novelties, there isn't one. He proclaimed his wares on uke-related instruments that grew bigger and louder as befitted his vaudeville and studio performances: the taro-patch, the banjulele (invented by our Hawaiian friends the Keech brothers) and latest in the line—the tiple, a ten-string uke with a faux but intriguing Latin American name.

In early 1924, the National Carbon Company signed "the Red Headed Music Maker" to host their *Eveready Hour* on WEAF in New York. They saluted him by having their batteries colored red. A champion of ballyhoo, Hall married his Chicago girlfriend Marion on the

Wendell Hall marrying Marion on the air at radio station WEAF.
From the collection of George Blau.

air at WEAF that winter. He was part of the big broadcast election broadcast hookup a few days later, sharing the spotlight with fellow cracker-barrel philosopher-entertainers Art Gillham ("The Whispering Pianist") and Will Rogers, the cowboy comedian and rope trickster. No doubt they recognized each other as professional Men of the People and exchanged knowing winks.

A ukulele empire began to grow with Hall's endorsement of the Wendell Hall signature Red Head Ukulele followed by a similar banjo-uke. Forster published his uke method, edited by Miss May Singhi Breen. Hall was making royalties by simply letting them use his name; he was too darned busy to work on designing ukes or editing songbooks. You gotta strike while it's hot—and he was off to England in 1925, following in the footsteps of Cliff Edwards, who'd played the London clubs the year before.

After that, his star began to fade, but he made a living in the 1930s writing copy for radio commercials. In 1950, because of Arthur Godfrey's resurrection of the ukulele via his radio and TV shows, Hall was offered a five-day-a-week TV show back in Chicago. His personalized ukes were sold once more and a new Wendell Hall method book was published. He was still writing songs, hoping for hits, right up until his death on April 2, 1969.

His records of the 1920s are a mixed bag, but worth listening to more than once. Hall was not a one-trick pony: he had another hit after "It Ain't Gonna Rain No Mo'," a ballad called "Mellow Moon," his own composition and rendered soft and croony. He did his bit with his fighting taro-patch on hits of the day like "Paddlin' Madelin' Home," but a lot of his output was self-written. He and his associate Carson Robison were early developers of the country style and form. As Robison explained to a British magazine in 1932: "After a while we started to worry about the well of original hill-billy songs going dry. The obvious answer to this was to educate the natives in a new type of song based on the old standards."

So we have Hall's "Toddlin' Along," set to a down-homey stroll, about a rover who, toting his load, travels the road apiece to his homeland down where the river bends: "Hallelujah! I'm comin' to ya!" Next he yearns (and goes into a late twenties trendy crooner murmur) to be in the "Land of My Sunset Dreams" set in days of long ago with his old sweetie same as ever. Quickly he's "Whistling the Blues Away" with virtuoso whistler Carson Robison. All the while, he's backed by in-demand New York players assigned to Wendell between sessions covering Broadway and Alley hits. Being versatile pros they sound like hillbillies except that they are actually in tune. As Robison went on to tell the magazine: "We still had to make simplicity our primary aim, because the backwoodsmen began to learn the new tunes from the records, and play them on their own crude instruments."

On "Headin' Home (Bound for Birmingham)," Hall is the engineer hectoring his passengers about the joys in store as he blows lonesome train whistles, chuff-chuffs, and makes his taro-patch sound like racing wheels. In all his perambulations, The Pineapple Picador had never ventured to this Deep South city where the good old days of slavery were still mourned and where overweening black carpetbaggers had not been forgotten or forgiven. Certain folks would not be at ease in the reality of this dreamscape, as Shelton Brooks, black writer of "Some of These Days" and "The Darktown Strutters' Ball," told me: "Man!—that was not a place you'd like to make a false move in unless you had a burning desire to be barbecued alive."

Yet, the music is good and the strumming is strong, and I feel certain that Wendell Hall would, if called upon, have placed himself at the head of a ukulele army and marched through the South in order to bring peace and understanding through the power of four strings on a pineapple!

JOHNNY MARVIN

Subdued and civilized almost to the point of blandness, Johnny Marvin was the most musicianly of our 1920s heroes, the best uke player, a multimillion-record seller, an A&R man and arranger for westerns, and the writer of a song nominated for an Academy Award: "Dust."

While Wendell Hall's stage persona verged on that of the buckaroo—he liked to don a tall Stetson when in an intimidating mood—Johnny Marvin's background, had he wanted to flaunt it, could have trumped the Kansan tenderfoot with ease, because he was the real rootsy thing in full color. The foreground, however, presented a pleasant-faced crooner in a dinner jacket with a microphonic voice that was the quintessence of the late Jazz Age, a flapper's delight.

He was born in 1897 in a covered wagon in the Oklahoma Territory, which then was still half-Indian and not yet a state in the Union. Nigh on two years previous, his parents, John and Molly, with a stake in government land, had left Missouri and now baby John Jr. appeared at the end of the trail, a few miles from Butler, a tiny town serving the farming community.

After a tough time ranching (brother Frankie was born in a dugout), his father tried realty, farm loans, and insurance. He built a nice house in Butler and in the evenings he and his wife made music on fiddle and accordion respectively. When Johnny was in his teens, his father had him play backup guitar at local gatherings and dances. Johnny didn't like his dad taking all the money, and there were other things too that irked him in that pent-up small town. So he ran away and joined a circus, came home, and ran away again. This last time he was gone for years and never wrote home.

In fact around 1915 in Bowlegs, Oklahoma, a rough-and-ready place settled by displaced Seminole Indians, he'd joined an itinerant group calling themselves the Royal Hawaiians, a bunch of fake islanders cashing in on the current craze for steel guitars, ukuleles, and grass skirts. Marvin now browned-up both his hair and skin and learned to play the uke and sing the Alley songs. In 1918 he joined the Navy, serving on land in San Diego as a crew barber.

As the 1920s began to roar, he went into a vaudeville troupe specializing in peppy jazz songs and dances, but not so as to offend. In 1921, passing through Butler, the local newspaper described the act as "renowned" and as purveying "some high-class music." By this time Johnny was not only playing the uke, but also the steel guitar, Jew's harp, and musical saw or "Arkansas fiddle." He sang sweetly if rather ordinarily. By 1925, the New York trade papers were taking notice, likening him to Ukulele Ike as well as noting his yodeling, though this, as *The Billboard* pointed out, " . . . like the singing, [was] not of an unusual sort." He was not striking in delivery like Ike or Wendell—although, as *The Billboard* credited, "His strong forte is playing the uke, which he picks in a mean manner."

It was this and his ability to make a kazoo-like noise with his voice that recommended

Marvin the elegant—a flapper's delight.

Marvin to dime-store record labels anxious to find someone who could imitate the pistol-hot Ike. Johnny was a king of pseudonyms: Elton Spence and His Ukulele, Ukulele Luke, Jack Lane and His Uke, plain George Thorne, and Billy Hancock, etc.—and Honey Duke and His Uke, the longest lasting.

As Duke Uke he played in a successful Broadway show in 1926 called *Honeymoon Lane*, also a debut for Kate Smith. He won encores and was praised for his "yelping," as well as his "trusty ukulele and untrusty vocal chords." He must have been "eefin'" like Cliff Edwards.

The show, which continued into 1927, got him a contract with the mighty Victor Records, also home to current stars "Whispering" Jack Smith and Gene Austin, exemplars of the fashionable intimate style that came to be known as "crooning." Victor was also noticing, from 1928, the phenomenal sales of hillbilly Jimmie Rodgers, "America's Blue Yodeler."

Marvin had all the attributes of a good ole country boy like Austin (who was a Texan), but the money at the moment was on the crooners, suave fellows who had close relations with the microphone, resulting in a bedside manner for the ladies. Victor, since the coming of electric recording, had been pruning away their beefy old belters like Billy Murray and Henry Burr. No more beer and sawdust; now it was cocktails ands canapés. Johnny Marvin had his timing right. A voice for the era: polished, likeable, and nonthreatening.

For two years he was a turntable favorite, cutting many kinds of pop from Gershwin tunes to best-selling covers of Ukulele Ike's "Singin' in the Rain" and Nick Lucas' "Tiptoe Through the Tulips." The Harmony Musical Instruments Company of Chicago produced a "Johnny Marvin Professional Tenor Ukulele" for $15 and a more expensive model made of Hawaiian koa wood, which they called "The Prince of Wales."

He took a custom-made version of the koa to London with him when he played the famous Kit Kat Club. The actual Prince of Wales, who had already sat in on drums with Paul Whiteman's band, was mad about the uke and the demented squirrel vocalizing that went with it. Right after his weekly strum lesson with Kelvin Keech, the prince dropped in to catch Marvin at the club and stood still long enough to be presented with his gift from Harmony—gold-plated uke with his coat of arms engraved on it. Not forgetting the commoners, Marvin and his new manager set about distributing the ten thousand disposable Harmony mini ukes they had brought with them.

The recording star phenomenon came home to read in the press that Victor was boasting about the constant spinning of ten million Johnny Marvin records in the households of America.

Meanwhile back in Butler, his kid brother Frankie had developed a nice knack with steel guitar and yodel. Soon, encouraged by Johnny, he was in New York and making Jimmie Rodgers copycat records for a host of labels. There were at least four versions of his cover of Rodgers's hit "Blue Yodel No. 1."

Frankie had a much more pronounced Okie twang than Johnny and was antsy and full of pep, altogether an animated character and thus a good fit for the Marvin Bros. in their vaudeville act. With his squashy-faced mugging and skilled steel guitar, he added a voguish rustic extra to his brother's rather straight-faced crooning. Frankie lived up to the accepted good ole boy down-hominess, drinking and cussing and jumping about.

So when a young fellow Oklahoman, a railroad worker called Gene Autry, hit New York and called up Johnny on the recommendation of the Marvins' mother, Molly, the record star took the call in a friendly way. The kid Gene breathlessly told of how swell their mother was looking and how well the café was doing—plastered with photos and clippings of Johnny—and how he, Gene, was a singer himself and looking to make it . . .

Johnny politely interrupted to suggest he room with Frankie, more his age and also hustling mad.

Autry was grateful and soon became Frankie's best friend and good-time partner, swinging with him through poolrooms and speakeasies and then returning to their room for all-night jams and beer, with the dead soldier bottles being tossed out the high window.

The Manger Hotel was a freewheeling place full of fellow entertainers in the rural record biz like Frank Luther and Vernon Dalhart. Autry bumped into Gene Austin, who was free with advice and flattered when the kid told him he'd changed his real first name Orvon to Gene in homage to his crooner idol. What's more, he said, he'd been using the urbane Austin ballad hit "Jeannine, I Dream of Lilac Time" as his audition number. "You carry on, kid," said Austin. "But do yourself a favor and go buy some fancier duds." The pudgy boy looked like the devil in blue serge.

Autry was crazy about Al Jolson too and had added "Sonny Boy" to his audition repertoire when he called at the record companies. He tried doing it onstage too till the Marvins nixed it, advising him to go back home and study Jimmie Rodgers and yodeling.

When he returned for another try at getting a recording contract, Johnny arranged for a test at a Victor studio. With Frankie backing on guitar and Johnny on steel, Autry sang a ballad written by the brothers and then an Alabammy song by Gene's pal Jimmy Long, a fellow railroader. Victor, logging the recordings as "Native American Melodies" accompanied by "two Hawaiian guitars," was in no hurry to release the sides. So, the determined Autry went off to cut a slew of rustic sides for cheap labels, frequently accompanied by Frankie.

Johnny was riding high as a star in May 1929, when he was billed equally in a nationwide radio broadcast with fellow crooners Frank Crumit, Gene Austin, and Rudy Vallée together with four massed orchestras directed by Nat Shilkret of Victor Records.

In 1930, when the great Wall Street crash was fresh, the ever kindly and helpful Johnny introduced Autry to "Uncle" Art Satherley. A veteran record man who mixed his own secret shellac formula, he was now a talent scout and producer at the American Record Company, a conglomerate of dime-store labels bought by Herbert Yates, whose main money came from Consolidated Film Industries, a processing plant for Hollywood studios. Uncle Art, a gentleman of the old school, trusted Johnny and was aware of the brothers' authentic country pedigrees. He also admired Johnny's well-cut business suits, for he himself was always neatly turned out, usually in creamy white suits with a well-placed tumbling pocket handkerchief. He was privately shocked by Autry's cheap suit.

Although his speech was dignified and tempered with a quaint burr (he hailed from Bristol, England), Satherley had in his time

**A garlanded Johnny Marvin
at the height of his career.**
Courtesy of Gene Autry Entertainment.

produced discs by earthy black blues artists like Ma Rainey and Blind Lemon Jefferson. At present he was tuned in to the busy market for hillbilly records, made cheaply, sold cheaply (three for a dollar at ARC), and chock full of sentiments kept close to the ground, but not quite the gutter.

Uncle Art was fond of telling how country music originated back in his homeland—why, even the blues could be traced to English peasants of Shakespeare's time. He liked to round off his dissertation by singing in a deep basso profundo voice "In the Cowslip Gardens Down

Autographed to his buddy Gene Autry by Johnny Marvin when he was the bigger star.
Courtesy of Gene Autry Entertainment.

in Cornwall" to the tune of "Trail of the Lonesome Pine (In the Blue Ridge Mountains of Virginia)." You could hear a pin drop, and that was the case the day Johnny Marvin and Autry were entertained. But Uncle Art meant business: he was to launch this other Oklahoma boy into fame and fortune.

First of all he recorded Autry on the nostalgic and regretful "That Silver-Haired Daddy of Mine" to a melody borrowed from the ever reliable "Red River Valley." Frankie Marvin supplied steel guitar. Autry cannily claimed the copyright. This would be his first hit, a huge one, and it was augmented by regular appearances on WLS radio's *National Barn Dance* in Chicago, the powerful plug all the rustic performers were clamoring to be on.

Satherley had been urging the hillbilly singer to metamorphose into the cowboy image, a much more romantic one than overalls and straws sticking out of the hair. The cowboy, despised in the old century as a ruffian, was now, thanks to the movies and pulp novels, pictured as a knight on horseback. Everyone who was into being powerful knew that. Presidents since Teddy Roosevelt understood that wearing a cowboy hat protected them from being considered effete or a stuffed shirt. "Four-square fellows on the move wear the ten-gallon!" pronounced Uncle Art with finality. Johnny Marvin agreed and got Autry some advice on how to look stylishly western for the WLS broadcasts, which were staged like big musical revues, except that millions at home everywhere could listen in and imagine. Autry's adviser, who'd been on the show as a stage buckaroo in Otto Gray's Oklahoma Cowboys, told him to wear decent and clean hat and boots and never, never tuck your pants inside your boots.

Autry took it all in and ordered a custom cowboy suit sent up from Hollywood. He was soon on his way to the Big Time. The final send-off into the stratosphere as the Singing Cowboy of the silver screen would take place in Southern California at Republic Pictures, maker of cheap mass dreams, another Herbert Yates enterprise. But the Autry rocket had been nurtured in New York by the Marvin brothers. Was there room for them now in a phantom empire of the silver screen presided over by a remote and almost portly Singing Cowboy?

The Great Depression had hit the record industry hard. Sales took a nosedive and Johnny Marvin's sunny disposition and period voice seemed old hat. The bounce of the uke was not wanted on the grim voyage; the plod of the guitar was in. Johnny, proficient on regular guitar as well as steel, was pinned forever as Honey Duke and His Uke. In those days, fashions in the pop world changed even faster than today. Unless you were secure in the western music scene where nostalgia still clicked, there was no time for the past, especially for Jazz Age "vo-do-de-o." The uke stood for silliness. Martin's uke sales fell to a measly 737 in 1933. In 1926 they'd been at 14,000.

The Marvin brothers were still working away in vaudeville, a dying business. In 1930, *The Billboard* reviewed their act at the Palace Theatre in New York and pinpointed the certain something that prevented Johnny from becoming a star, as well as spotlighting Frankie's talents.

"Maybe Marvin is a big guy in disc recording, but as a vaudeville single he lacks plenty. Fortunately the personable but pep-deficient artiste does not attempt to go it alone." Frankie, on the other hand, playing a typical rustic boob in green shoes, sausage-shaped suit, and back-woods haircut, "sells himself well" with "more appealing pipes than his better-known brother—and he knows his yodels."

Gene Autry, now the peacemaker of celluloid pop culture—with both his guns and soothing personality—hadn't forgotten the help, friendship, and artistic usefulness of the Marvin brothers. By 1937, Frankie and Johnny were both settled with their wives near Republic Pictures as hardworking employees of the Autry Empire. Frankie played on the soundtracks and appeared in some of the pictures; Johnny arranged and supervised those recordings, as well as producing the *Melody Ranch* radio shows and partnering with Autry in Western Music Publishing Company. Johnny also wrote more

than seventy songs for the pictures, often collaborating with Tin Pan Alley and Chicago veteran Fred Rose, who in the 1920s had made records in the prevailing smooth crooning style to his own effective piano. Both Fred and Johnny knew how to combine down-home folksiness with Alley slickness and all bottled tightly in fully tested song forms.

Johnny was tied to the Autry clan as loyal friend and employee. He even, like Fred Rose and others in the social circle, joined with Mrs. Autry and became a Christian Scientist.

After the Pearl Harbor sneak attack, Mr. and Mrs. Fred Rose, fearing a Japanese invasion, fled to Nashville, where Fred set up what was to be a very successful publishing company with hillbilly star Roy Acuff. In contrast, Autry joined the army and became a sergeant and Johnny did his bit by joining the USO and touring bases in the South Pacific, singing his old hits to troops who barely remembered him and lusted for girl performers. In Papua, he contracted dengue fever and could have been successfully treated, but his religious beliefs forbade interference by humankind. He returned to his home in North Hollywood and died there of a heart attack on December 10, 1944.

A tiny paid-for obituary was printed in the *Los Angeles Times* and *The New York Times*. There was nothing else.

Johnny Marvin made some very satisfying records that go beyond the confines of the Jazz Age. His instrumental take on "12th Street Rag," a test for technique, shows him to be a master of a syncopation trick where the audience thinks too many notes are crowding into the bar space yet the effect is jolting and thrilling ("da dada di dada"). Having a guitarist supplement and help with the second and more

The title page from "The Old Trail" sheet music. Note the unique rope border—emblematic of Autry's attention to detail.
Courtesy of Gene Autry Entertainment.

difficult chorus was a good idea; Marvin knew that the uke alone was not enough.

His work with small and loose jazz-like ensembles in numbers such as "From Sunset Till Dawn" and "Melancholy" is exemplary as a benchmark of late twenties strum 'n' croon. Regular guitar, steel guitar, string bass, and uke make a perfect blend—I wish that virtuoso wizards realized this truth.

The voice is unwaveringly tuneful and merry—never disturbing; the uke playing is disciplined and straight ahead with no ornamentation, no finger-flicking rolls to distract or interfere with the rhythmic forging-ahead.

Marvin, like Ukulele Ike, has a troubling habit of sometimes garbling the harmony, thus leaving out enriching secondary chords that are in the original piano arrangement. He does this in "Me and My Shadow," where the uke sticks out because he's with a very small group. He recorded this same 1927 hit with the mighty Victor Orchestra conducted by Nat Shilkret, and here he's supported by all the right harmonies and the uke on the vocal refrain is sprightly and cushioned by well-trained band boys, thus another perfect blend avoiding the tediousness of the naked lone uke.

That same year, 1927, Johnny's best, saw him cowriting songs. The guy who raised laughs with "Oh, How She Could Play a Ukulele!" and "My Wife's in Europe" showed he knew the potency of the old verities and images: "An Old Fashioned Locket," recorded by Wendell Hall in his best new crooner voice, contains a tintype of a girl together with her curl, and the two nostalgic objects produce a silent tear from the old lover who regrets the long and empty years. A good tune with a Victorian sentiment still appealing to the emerging rural audience—anything old remained surefire with that certain segment, as Johnny found in his Hollywood cowboy years: "The Old Trail," written with Fred Rose for use in an Autry western, has our hero riding "o'er" the prairie to his old girl in the hope that she's still waiting. The tune is a standard Alley heart-tugger and all the better for that. In another Rose collaboration, "I'm Beginning to Care," the seasoned songwriters cunningly call up echoes of an old hit waltz, "My Wonderful One," for their melody.

However, in "Dust," which Johnny wrote alone, there's a refreshing originality in its minor-key plaintiveness and extensive and well-planted diminished chords. The Lord is called upon to intercede with rain and sunshine; the whole drama has a sort of Wagnerian *Sturm* atmosphere about it. The song, sung by Roy Rogers in *Under Western Stars* (in lieu of Autry, who was having a pay dispute with Republic), was nominated for an Academy Award in 1938.

Johnny Marvin, the Oklahoma kid, was up there with the big Broadway and Hollywood names, having brought the lessons of old-time Tin Pan Alley to modern Western heroes who might be on horseback one moment and in a streamlined car or plane the next.

MAY SINGHI BREEN—OUR HEROINE

Our lone heroine, at least in the USA, worked behind the scene. You never see her face much, but her name as uke arranger seems to be on every piece of pop sheet music from the Jazz Age onwards. She was our evangelist, our advocate, and our matronly booster. She fought like mad for decades to get our instrument accepted as legitimate. She was way ahead of her time in promulgating the idea of the ukulele as a magnet for community strum-along sing-alongs

May Singhi Breen.
From the collection of Flea Market Music.

BACK VIEW

"Sweethearts of the Air"—May Singhi Breen accompanied by her husband, Peter DeRose.
From the collection of Flea Market Music.

and get-togethers that might result in lasting friendships or even romances. She'd be leading the uke crusade today, and with that South Seas-sounding middle name, she might pass as a Hawaiian authentic.

But she wasn't from the islands. Her family came from Maine and she was born in the New York of the Gay Nineties. As a child, she learned piano and later banjo. As a young woman she married an attorney called Breen who, after they parted, got himself murdered; as a thirty-year-old divorcée she was adrift with a daughter, a little money, and lots of time on her hands. In 1922, when Hawaiian bands were still roaming in vaudeville and Edwards, Crumit, and Marvin were establishing the uke as a signature pop sound, May Singhi was given a cheap one as a Christmas present. Unsuccessful at trying to exchange it at the store for a bathrobe, she decided to have a bash at the thing. Like so many before and after, she fell in love with the dinky creature. Then, like a missionary, she went proselytizing and eventually rounded up friends into an all-girl group she called the Syncopators. Pleasingly plump, with rosy-pink cheeks, Breen charmed a local radio station to let her gals do a few tunes as a novelty.

Next year she was on the air as a soloist at WEAF in New York as The Ukulele Lady (the song had become a hit). Here she met Peter DeRose, a spruce and stylish little man, twelve years her junior, with a pencil mustache and a Frenchified manner. He played flowery piano and was working for the longhair Italian music publisher G. Ricordi & Co., home of Puccini. However, he wrote accessible and successful pop on the side, and he was entranced by the spirited May Singhi and her fiery mission.

She'd been pestering the Alley publishers

May Singhi Breen with her P'Mico autographed model banjo-uke.
From the collection of Flea Market Music.

Uke Method. This was followed by other teaching books, including a six-minute course complete with a demo record (the first ukulele instructional record—a 78 rpm Victor label record titled *Ukulele Lesson*). She had great hopes for elevating the uke above mere strumming and propagated her slogan: "Uke Can Play the Melody." Few listened—they were more interested in being entertainers like our uke crooners.

By this time, she and Peter were married and were radio stars as *The Sweethearts of the Air,* a show that lasted sixteen years. Her uke demonstrations were so popular with listeners that there soon was a May Singhi Breen P'Mico autographed model banjo-uke on sale everywhere.

While DeRose was writing hits like "Somebody Loves You," "Have You Ever Been Lonely?" "Wagon Wheels," and eventually "Deep Purple," with its great roller-coaster melody worthy of grand opera, Breen was teaching away at her stu-

to add uke chords to their songs, because fewer and fewer customers were learning piano since more and more were turning passive due to the phonograph and the radio. With a uke, she reasoned, you could master a Schubert song and a Berlin was child's play. The Alley listened and hired her to "arrange," which really meant putting in the sheet music, just above the melody line, a grid with dots showing where the fingers are to press on the fretboard. Breen didn't invent this—there are variants reaching back to Hawaiian methods of the early 1900s—but she did refine the grid to the point of utter simplicity.

Breen and DeRose teamed up as singer-songwriters and he helped with the publication of her first do-it-yourself uke book: *The Peter Pan*

Hundreds of thousands of people learned from Breen's method books.
From the collection of Flea Market Music.

dio and tirelessly promoting. The uke, she wrote, should be an essential in schools, scout camps, and old-folks' homes. "Group playing leads to enjoyment for young and old." And, indeed, she was the first to teach ukulele in schools.

She was furious when, in 1932, the American Federation of Musicians refused her entry as a ukulele player, stating that her joy was a "lowly instrument," no more than a "fun toy." To the rumble of noble Hawaiians rolling in their graves she went up to see the union bosses, flashing her expensive ($135) instrument and demanding to know why they accepted harmonica and triangle players and not her people. Then she gave the startled men a short concert. Still no go. They told her she might be admitted as a pianist—but not with this wretched toy.

Breen and DeRose recorded this song by Haven Gillespie who also cowrote songs with DeRose.

Time magazine noted her troubles humorously, but *The Washington Post* demanded " . . . that all ukulele players be refused membership on the grounds that a ukulele player is anything in the world but a musician and that this music box, so-called, is really an instrument of torture."

Undaunted, she enlisted the help of famous conductor Walter Damrosch, a radio star himself, inspiring him to describe her playing as: "delightful—charming—like raindrops in sunshine." Husband Peter went further and wrote a symphonic poem for her entitled "Inspiration." Paul Whiteman conducted his orchestra behind her picking the rhapsody at Aeolian Hall—where, almost a decade before, George Gershwin's "Rhapsody in Blue" had premiered with the same orchestra and conductor. Despite the highbrow campaign, the AFM refused to budge.

Even so, ASCAP honored the DeRose and Breen partnership in 1940 by including them in a cheerleading concert at San Francisco's Coliseum, an event designed to propagandize the belief that the society's composers and authors were the true creators of America's music, and not the hillbillies and bluesmen the radio interests were threatening to foist onto an unsuspecting public. Peter played a semiclassical arrangement of his "Deep Purple," raining down showers of impressive notes for high art gravitas. But then, making things a bit more human, Breen joined him on the concert stage with her best ukulele and the two sweetly sang three of Peter's hits in two-part harmony. Fifteen thousand roared their approval as The Ukulele Lady's strings had the last word, ringing out into the night air to tell the world the good news.

During World War II, she served as national director of air-raid precautions for the

American Women's Voluntary Services, as well as being associate director of the New York Air Warden Service. *Zoftig* and commanding, she always had her uke by her side and liked to thrust it into the night sky as a warning to the Nazis and, perhaps, to the AFM.

Branch by branch they relented, starting with Los Angeles (under pressure from Cliff Edwards), until finally in the early 1950s, with major help from radio exposure by Arthur Godfrey, all the branches gave in, accepting the once lowly toy as a bona fide musical instrument. Breen was still in the business putting out method books: in 1950 she'd authored a comic-book version to be sold with the Maccaferri plastic *Sparkle Plenty Islander Ukette*, named after a character in the Dick Tracy comic strip. An added bonus was a book called *Godfrey the Great: The Life Story of Arthur Godfrey*, the radio personality who had singlehandedly revived dwindling uke sales.

May Singhi Breen, widowed since Peter DeRose's death in 1953, was still writing songs and singing the praises of the uke as a cure-all in 1970, the year of her death. It was a world enveloped in a hangover mushroom cloud of psychedelia mixed with heavy metal, smothering the shrill but worthy cries of Tiny Tim, a character she'd have embraced like an earth mother.

Note the songwriting and the publishing collaboration of Breen and DeRose.
From the collection of Flea Market Music.

CHAPTER FOUR

MEANWHILE IN ENGLAND....

GRINNING THROUGH THE GREAT DEPRESSION

GEORGE FORMBY JR.

We turn now to England and to a fish-faced banjo-uke player with an amazing world-beating strum and a thick-accented voice, chipped and compressed to a thin cry from the nostrils—no crooner he—who was a beloved performer in the British Empire and even Russia.

He's still unknown over here in the U.S., although I've done my best to educate audiences via radio and concert.

Some of his songs work fine without him, but generally you need the George Formby persona itself, the bedside manner of a mile-wide smile doctor. For the medicine to work, one must meet this odd creature head-on and embrace him like a Cheshire cat with tombstone teeth.

My wife, for example, had had a bad day, but that night I sat her in front of an imported Formby film, *Let George Do It*, and soon her peals of laughter filled the room and dull care fled screaming into the night.

"Our George," as his North Country brethren called him but I didn't dare to because I'm from the cushy soft South and from the upper class, wasn't just a local dish like a Lancashire hot pot. His relentless cheer-up slogan "It's Turned Out Nice Again" lit up a dark and stormy 1930s Britain, and his high-speed syncopated banjo-uke sped along saucy songs that, though deemed offensive by the BBC, gave much-needed relief and pleasure.

The rewards for George were many: between 1934 and 1946, through movies and recordings, he was Britain's biggest box-office star and the richest (about $10 million a year); the royal family, especially Queen Mary, adored him and commanded his presence at their homes; the government realized his importance as a morale booster in World War II and let him entertain as near to the guns as he liked; afterwards he was awarded the Order of the British Empire. He started recording in 1926 when Ukulele Ike was making it big; his last release, in 1960, almost joined Elvis in the charts—we embryonic British Invaders, from Beatle to Kink, loved the single, "Happy Go Lucky Me" with "Banjo Boy" on the other side. When he died the following year, he left a legacy of almost two hundred recordings and twenty-two starring movies.

One of his many Rolls Royces turned up in Los Angeles a few years ago and I was invited to take a look at the dashboard: an embossed notice in bold letters said, "George Formby, OBE." I'd heard that his banjo-ukes had a habit of turning up in odd parts of the world, including Arizona—the same with his ties and underwear. By this time I had loads of his recordings as well as a banjo-uke with his endorsement name stamped at the top. I was receiving royalty checks courtesy of my dead auntie for funny songs that my even-deader uncle had written for Formby at the start of his career. I was proud to have a tenuous (albeit quite lucrative) connection.

He'd permeated my life as far back as teendom when, as my schoolmates were drooling over the blue moans of Bessie Smith and King Oliver, I was mulling over a TV appearance by George in the holidays. My parents had kindly alerted me to the program. George was not really their cup of tea, of course, but they encouraged my pop obsession since I wasn't any good at sports.

The TV show featured a jaunty song called "You Don't Need a License for That" in which George's chirpy banjo-uke kept the orchestra on their feet and racing to catch up. I loved the way he'd break into a word with a chuckle. I recorded it on my new Grundig tape machine and played the song back over and over, but never could understand the line where he seemed to be saying, "We'll have a good time, a wives-in-the-wood time." What was the excitement of a wife in the wood? And then: "As Fred Bailey said when he looked at his wife, 'You don't need a license for that.'" Who was Fred or was it Ted? No matter—like a good abstract painting or a piece of Ravellian expressionism, the Formby spell cast logic and meaning to the four winds. You had to shed the deadly rational world to be transported.

My recording was indistinct but I learned the song word for word as best I could—religiously—and repeated it to my bemused school friends and stunned masters. Wrote my housemaster in the end-of-term report: "He seems keen on music—of a sort."

In the show there was a cheeky number I did understand—about the pleasures of hiking with his girl and how a "bumblebee there in the grass came and stung her on the . . . elbow." The words were ripe but there was also a nifty shock chord that I was dying to discover. And all I had at hand was a school piano, but pop or jazz were both prohibited at the time for interfering with exam preparation. I didn't bother to try and describe to boys or staff the magic of George. It was ineffable—easier to write about the Wars of the Roses, as I'd have to at the end of the term.

Luckily, during the summer holidays, I found a cheap uke at my cousin's house together with an EP called *The Ukulele Man* on which George sang four songs. Many of them had the shock chord as the penultimate flourish. I borrowed the uke, went home, looked up some 1920s sheet music and found the shock chord in context in "Bye Bye Blues": C to Ab and back to C again. I was on my way! And I didn't need to affect a Lancashire accent to perform stuff like George's "Hi-Tiddly Hi-Ti-Island," because it was written before his coming. I felt authentic, free to be myself.

If only my parents had not been sophisticated revue aficionados and had alerted me to George's 1959 summer season on Yarmouth Pier! My rock 'n' roll mentors Jerry Lee Lewis and Elvis were currently taking time out and the time would have been ripe for some uke education. Plus, our family was summering by the seaside in a posh country club setting only a few miles from Yarmouth. Culturally, though, we were a million miles away. I missed my chance!

Two years later George Formby was dead. But I took LPs of his work to Trinity College Dublin and played them secretly, waiting in the wings for the right moment to bring out the uke in public and spread a little happiness.

Within months of his death, a George Formby Society was founded with its own magazine, *The Vellum*, edited by Kevin Daly who, like me, had preferred Formby to the politically correct black jazz that his school friends hunched over. In the 1970s, Kevin, the keeper of the Formby flame with a complete collection of mint-condition 78s by our hero, produced an album of me and added his banjo-uke to one of the tracks. He had mastered the notoriously hard Formby split stroke and I marveled. He tried to teach me and failed. He died a few years later.

Today the George Formby Society flourishes, throwing an annual convention in Blackpool, Lancashire, scene of some of George's greatest triumphs and a setting for several of his songs. He was at his happiest and most serene in Blackpool-by-the Sea.

There the members, some from Scandinavia and others from as far away as Australia, swap little-known facts about their star and sign up to pay homage with imitations from the sacred repertoire. *The Vellum* wonders why certain songs are never attempted, listing "Kiss Your Mansy Pansy" and "I'm a Froggie" (cowritten by my Uncle Stanley), as well as such sketches as "John Willie at the License Office."

Both society and magazine are strictly for the devoted and learned: a quiz asks, "In what way was the Formby family associated with the Italian Royal Family?" (Answer: *George's uncle on his mother's side was head postilion to King Umberto*.) The winner of the *Wartime Recipe* book gets all the answers right, even "What did George's girl say when he showed her his new underwear?" (Answer: *A splendid fit—I must admit you've got something there*.") The letters page includes one from a Coldstream Guardsman representing six GFS members fighting the Taliban in Afghanistan: "We are with the Czech Special Forces and they aren't enjoying George much, but not to worry—we'll educate them!"

The society hopes that the current uke craze will continue indefinitely and attract new members. A clipping from *The Daily Telegraph*, a snooty Southern newspaper, tells of how the recorder, traditional instrument for musical youngsters in primary school, is being supplanted by the ukulele. "This news must certainly be applauded by members of the GFS." However, the paper goes on to regret the usurping, saying that the well-fingered and well-blown recorder "runs a straight road to Purcell and Vivaldi, who carelessly omitted to write works for the ukulele."

Yes, there are youngsters coming onstage to announce George's catchphrases "It's turned out nice again!" or "Eeh, isn't it grand!" followed by a ritual sticking out of the front teeth, before attempting "I'm the Husband of the Wife of Mr. Wu," but they are a minority beside the senior strummers. Will today's trendy cutting-edge youth, those who thrill to the mile-a-minute picking of flash uke prodigies, with their Charlie Parker and Jimi Hendrix adaptations, get turned on to Our George?

Years ago I went on a pilgrimage to Blackpool, accompanied by my wife and a sunbleached Californian husband-and-wife team. I led them to the very top of the city's famous tower. After looking at the desolate, windblown sand stretching flatly to a battle-gray and dead-still sea and then at the flapping posters of aging 1960s beat groups soon to appear here with one or two some original members, I broke out my Martin and performed "Spotting on the Top of Blackpool Tower." This epic contains two great couplets: one about a helpful girl fiddling with "my little telescope" and another about watching a buxom girl who's learning swimming only for the voyeur to discover that "the things that I thought water wings weren't water wings at all."

When we got safely home to my mother's luxury flat near Wimbledon, down south among the decadent rich, we told her of our adventure. She was horrified: "How could you subject unsuspecting Americans to such a common and vulgar hole as Blackpool!?"

⊙⊙⊙⊙⊙⊙⊙⊙⊙

Formby's North, into which he was born in 1904, was an industrial eyesore as well as being the crucible of Britain's wealth. Dark satanic cotton mills and coal mines, owned by men who knew that "where there's muck there's brass," produced the gold that went trundling down to the sybaritic South, leaving a foul and noxious land impolitely known as "the Arse-Hole of England."

The capital of ugliness was Wigan, Formby's birthplace in Lancashire, where the birds flew backwards to keep the coal dust out of their eyes. Things were much the same in the late 1930s when George Orwell, rigged up in a workingman's costume made by his London tailor, arrived in the dirty old town for some investigative. He described a "lunar landscape of slag-heaps," of "factory chimneys sending out plumes of smoke" and of "pools of stagnant water." Altogether a "world from which vegetation has been banished; nothing existed except smoke, shale, ice, mud, ashes, and foul water."

The book's title, *The Road to Wigan Pier*, was borrowed from an ironic joke by Formby's father, a music hall star in the teen years of the century. For this pier, long demolished by the time Orwell came, had been no glittering fun palace pointing out over the sea into the blue horizon like a bejeweled finger beckoning to a brilliant land beyond. It was just a wooden jetty over a noxious canal built for coal loading, and most days it was shrouded in smog.

George Formby Sr., clever artist that he was, told in his act of the wonders to be seen on his invented Wigan Pier, of the giant and tasty fish to be caught and of the wiggle-walk of fashionable women. "Ah've bin there many a time in me bathing costume and dived off high board inta water . . . Don't laugh, it's all true . . . Song, please."

The comic song was the solid rock of all music hall acts from the beginning of time: Song—patter jokes—song (with maybe some eccentric step dance, or a clog shoe dance if you were from up North).

His son would, in the 1930s, take up the droll myth and sing of riding "The Wigan Boat Express." Upon arrival, one could take in the sea air—the real town was in fact landlocked—on the promenade or dally "In a Little Wigan Garden" where crocuses croak with the gas and the smoke from the gas works and the only thing that grows is the wart on his sweetie's nose. "A disgrace to my hometown!" sings George. This social-realism of the muckraking kind was obliterated by the next picture in the song—of George with girl on knee showing how his rhubarb grows.

His father, stalwart of the halls, never sang "suggestive." Taking his carefully drawn stage character from the Northern tradition of helpless simpletons or Wet Willies, he presented himself as "John Willie," a man-boy thrust into this wicked world when he'd much rather be safe at home with mother. Young women either terrified or dominated him. There was never any question of sex. John Willie sometimes found himself in London and he'd boast of not going home till a quarter to ten "'cos it's my night out!" Although he posed as a fast swell out on the spree and knocking the policemen about, his stage clothes told another story. Wearing a baggy suit that had seen better days and clobber boots that were too big and with a vacuous expression on his face, he was the epitome of what Northerners termed a "gormless gowk." There were other Northern comedians, like Tom Foy and Jack ("I'm Shy, Mary Ellen, I'm Shy") Pleasants, playing this stock character that Southerners adored—the equivalent of the simple darky Dixie minstrel in America—but Formby perfected him, taking his time onstage, building him slowly and filling him out.

He'd enter the stage tentatively, cast

around for the conductor, and tell him he was "coughing better tonight." (In truth he was suffering from tuberculosis and bronchitis contracted during his early days working brutal alehouses when he was plain Jimmy Booth.) He'd chat awhile with the musicians about this new ragtime and other insects, before recognizing his audience. He'd deliver for them a bigger cough: "That was a good one, best I've had this year." How they roared, little knowing. Between songs he'd descend into the stalls to exchange a few pleasantries with the people. Were they as good as him at coughing? He understood. "Be kind to me, please—I haven't been in England long." Just offstage, in the wings, was an oxygen tent at the ready in case of breathing problems, provided by his protective wife, Eliza.

They loved him for his slow way, he took his time, no flurry hurry like these Yankee ragtimers who, in the 1910s, were rudely invading the theaters. He played for the royals both at command performances and privately. He was a favorite among his peers. And the kid Charlie Chaplin studied him carefully, noting the way he swished his cane when playing a nob on the town. Formby was making a lot of money and bought big impressive houses up North and later a string of racehorses. George Jr. was kept strictly away from the stage business, never allowed to see his father work. "One fool in the family's enough," he was told.

Instead, noting his son's love of animals, George Sr. packed him off to be a jockey. Maybe eventually his number-one son might run the family stable. Boy George didn't care much for the racing life. He'd rather be playing his father's records or the mouth organ or humming into comb-and-paper. Schooling was intermittent—he never learned much about reading and writing. He was unable to write letters home and couldn't read the ones he received. He was very lonely. He had a rough gamin look. Not unattractive.

Sometimes his father, in search of new comic songs, took him to London's Tin Pan Alley, showing off the boy jockey to the trade. Lawrence Wright, an up-and-coming publisher and songwriter, who later was to publish the son's hit songs, was visited. "George is crazy about horses," said the father, uncharacteristically employing an American expression. George grinned sheepishly but didn't agree. He was looking longingly at the bright and gaudy covers of the ragtime songs lying on Mr. Wright's desk—songs like "I Want to Go Back to Michigan," and "Back to the Carolina You Love."

Mr. Wright said not to worry about the Yank rag stuff—he had a gang of writers right here in London, men like Tom Mellor and Harry Gifford, who could pump out the rags every bit as good as the Yanks. Had father and son heard their current "Don't Say Goodbye Miss Ragtime," let alone their hit ballad "Shine on Harvest Moon," which they'd sold to a New York vaudeville act called Bayes and Norworth back in 1909? Hadn't George Sr. himself recorded British-made songs about cakewalk, and didn't he right now have a record called "John Willie's Ragtime Band" describing mill girls flocking round them when they play on Wigan Pier as the colliers shout, "By gum! Itchy koo! Itchy koo!"? Aye, one in the eye to those upstart Americans!

That was in 1914. After the Great War settled down to be a long one, George Jr. was packed off to Ireland for more of the same with the horses. Every now and then he'd return

George Formby

Formby with banjulele.
Courtesy of Michael Daly, georgeformby.org.

and again be paraded in London. Mr. Wright tried to get his father to put a new effort by Mellor and Gifford into his act, an up-to-date novelty called "All Going Back," a comment on those American songs like "Back Home in Tennessee." The English song made father and son laugh and it had a punch-line ending: "But there's only one thing worries me: when they all get back to Tennessee there'll be no one left in Wigan but me!"

Father Formby said he'd take a copy and mull it over. Wright added that a royalty cut and writing credit deal could be struck. The song was introduced into the act during a Christmas pantomime at the Empire Newcastle in 1920.

His first hit.
From the collection of Ian Whitcomb.

Boy George was still jockeying in Ireland when, next year, his father had a coughing fit onstage at that same theater and died a week later.

೧೧೧೧೧೧೧೧

The Jazz Age was in full swing. The American Invasion was knocking out steady old rude but stately Music Hall. The Original Dixieland Jazz Band had amazed London and local bands were scrambling to emulate them. The Hawaiian-born Keech brothers, Alvin and Kelvin, abandoning Los Angeles, had relocated in England, setting up a ukulele shop in London, manufacturing their patented banjo-uke invention and selling it as a "banjulele."

Soon concert party and revue performers were spotlighting these cheap and strident instruments in their acts. Kelvin Keech had a sideline job with Feldman's, the West End publishers, placing uke chord grids into their piano arrangements. By 1921, he'd perfected a system he'd learned from his Hawaiian brothers back on the islands—he was way ahead of May Singhi Breen. Up in Monmouthshire, Bill and Doris Harley—concert uke and banjo-uke—wore leis as they brought Hawaiian sunshine to this rainy region. Like jazz, ukes were infiltrating everywhere.

Here's a puzzle in the senior Formby's story: the father left over a million dollars, yet Eliza, the mother, was right away dressing her sixteen-year-old son in the dead man's stage costume and using her contacts to get him gigs. Eliza later explained that she had to put the eldest boy to work because she was short of cash and had seven kids to support. The boy himself said he nearly starved that year. So what happened to all the money?

There's a true story that George Sr. was a bigamist and a not-proven story that a first wife called Martha got all the fortune.

Be that as it may, the new George Formby was on his way, though at first the road was rocky. He really didn't want to tread the boards, but mother must be obeyed—the first lady in a life dominated by females. She rehearsed him on the old songs and patter, but this wasn't hard work because he'd learned them voluntarily much earlier. She had him billed under her maiden name as "George Hoy" with the subtitle "Son of the Late George Formby." She bribed theater owners who'd loved the father, and had box office receipts to prove it, to book this "chip off the old block." They agreed so long as the name was straightened out.

So he was now George Formby Jr., stumbling along with his father's material and getting the boot, the egg, and the bird. "I died the death of a dog," he said. No amount of help from his father's old bookers could get audiences to accept him. In fact, they resented him.

As a change from being a pale ghost, his manager-mother wangled Georgie into a minstrel show where he could hide himself in blackface and strum a new toy as he sang "All Going Back," an appropriate number.

The toy was a Kelvin Keech banjulele bought on impulse at junk shop in Manchester. He'd been tootling through in his new air-cooled Rover, a present from his mother (who seems to have located some of that inheritance money) when he spotted it. As a typically fidgety teenager he loved all the latest jazzy pop songs. Although he didn't read music, he could understand the new uke grids—saw where you "finger-stopped" on the fret. He paid fifteen shillings for the battered juvenile banjo with the dirty vellum and was soon having a bash at it. You could get a decent percussive ring and a few basic chords within minutes. No wonder other acts were adopting the banjulele. His voice matched as if born to be together—a righteous clang-clatter.

Being a good mother's boy he stuck to his father's repertoire—the lugubrious, now almost baleful mishaps in waltz-time like "The Man Was a Stranger to Me," in which he's robbed of his gold watch in one verse and invited into a young lady's parlor in the next, and when she offers him a pastry he flees in terror.

He was doing right by his mother, with the Tennessee uke song sandwiched in the middle of the act and a string of parrot jokes elsewhere, when he met the woman who changed his direction, setting him on the right road to stardom.

Beryl Ingham, trim-figured and pretty and a few years his senior, was in a tap-dancing sister act on the same bill. She watched his sorry farrago in horror: "If I'd had a bag of rotten tomatoes, I'd have thrown them." It was all so dated and deathly. The glory of music hall was over.

But the uke song impressed her and she liked his naughty-boy looks and the well-muscled jockey body. She liked the sparkling eyes that radiated innocence, as if he'd just been dropped by the stork and was bewildered by what he saw down here below. It didn't take long for the couple to click, and in 1924 they were married. Mother Eliza, seeing a rival, refused to attend. She'd spent a lot of money pushing her boy, but in the wrong direction.

Beryl took over and George didn't mind. He'd rather be tinkering with cars or listening to the latest records by Frank Crumit and Ukulele Ike now being released in Britain. That's the ticket, said Beryl. Get to be as good as they are on the ukulele. He practiced and practiced, driving his fellow performers to distraction. If only Kelvin Keech could give him a few pointers—but he was down in the ritzy South, giving lessons to the Prince of Wales and others of that ilk.

In 1926, Eliza persuaded the small Winner label to let her son lay down a few of his father's songs, as well as some written by Stanley Damerell (my uncle) and his partner Bob Hargreaves, who'd worked with George Sr. in the old days. "John Willie's Jazz Band" is a follow-up to the 1914 ragtime number. The band is on the pier again and this time blowing so rotten that the people "fill their ears with sand"; when playing near a "cook shop" they manage to turn "black puddings white with fear." The recordings are eerie: they sound like they were made in 1914—tinny and with the same arrangements. Beryl despaired. She and George toiled on in tatty revues, she tapping nicely and he coasting along with the same old dad-nostalgia and a few new parrot jokes.

In 1927, Johnny Marvin's "12th Street Rag" instrumental was released and George closely studied the syncopated three-over-four melody lick in the opening bars that Marvin used to great effect. He mastered it in the C key positions and the trick, fashioned into a special sound that in the end was all his own, became the basis of the Formby rhythm solo style. He

never learned to differentiate keys and only collected banjo-ukes so as to have each one tuned to the particular key for the particular song. He wrote "low key" or "high" on the case. After he became a big star in the 1930s, he had the banjo-ukes laid out in a grand array onstage. It all looked very impressive unless you were a stagehand and could see that each one was named with the song it was employed to play.

By 1929, his uke technique was near-perfected: the right hand doing the rhythmic strumming and the left alternating between stopping the fret and lifting off. That year he went back into the recording studio with Eliza's money and Beryl's supervision, this time for the Dominion label, another modest operation.

One of the songs was "All Going Back," and he imitated his father's humorous badinage with the conductor, leading the listener to believe nothing had changed and the boy's stuck in a copycat relic rut. But suddenly, in the last chorus, he goes into a triumphantly loud uke solo, skating over the stuttering rhythms of the ragtimey melody. The first flowering of a great clanking beauty bursts forth, albeit chunkily, casting a shadow over his father's comic but sad loser apparel and demeanor. From now on, the dancing rays of the banjo-uke solo would be standard on almost every recording by the "New" George Formby.

The new boy was firmly under the thumb of Beryl and Eliza. The Dominion records were flops, but the two loving and focused harpies turned their attention to George's stage presence before badgering the record people again. They paid a hefty sum to an impresario to throw the diffident lad into revues and Christmas pantomimes (family-friendly musical comedies based on fairy tales, spotted with

Rehearsing at the London Palladium, 1937.
Courtesy of Michael Daly, georgeformby.org.

vaudeville routines) as a support act in order to learn how to hold an audience—employing that full-toothed mile-long smile, the shy shuffling gait, and the banjo-uke. Now they needed new songs to complement the strum. Fast, funny, different. No more haplessness in three-quarter time.

While he was playing Billy Goose in a pantomime, as part of this expensive showbiz crash course, fellow Lancastrian and revue artist Jack Cotterill, who wrote special material and songs

on the side, visited him in his dressing room. George was busy in the middle of a class on comic timing, mugging, and goofy looks, so Cotterill just picked up one of the many labeled ukes lying around and started a novelty song he thought would be perfect for George.

"The Chinese Laundry Blues," jogging along steadily with a note for almost every beat and no syncopation, did have some of those Yankee blue crushed notes in keeping with modern times, but it was also local in that

me—waistcoat." This could be a winner, said George. Remember to add a reassuring wink, said the coach. Saucy double-meaning songs go down well with the boys in the band at the pub. Show it to Beryl.

Beryl, forceful and attractive woman, secured an audition for George at Decca Records, a proper label, in London at their Chenil Galleries studio. He passed. In 1932, Decca tried him on a session with the celebrated bandleader Jack Hylton, Britain's answer to Paul Whiteman. Jack had met the

it dealt with the "outlandish" yet mysterious Orientals settled in the Limehouse section of Liverpool.

Mr. Wu, the laundryman, has fallen for a Chinese girl and is neglecting his business so that our singer has contracted a "kind of Limehouse Chinese laundry blues." His new Sunday shirt has got a "perforated rudder." George was unimpressed until Cotterill reached a couplet about Mr. Wu's naughty eye that flickers: "You ought to see it wobble when he's ironing ladies—blouses . . . " He chuckled; so did the comedy coach. The next couplet told of Mr. Wu owning a business rather tricky: "He starched me shirt and collars, but he never touched

Formbys at a party and heard the Mr. Wu song. They might tuck it in on the date. The main number, chosen by Beryl, was to be "Do De O Do," a comment on American nonsensicals like "Crazy Words Crazy Tune (Vo-Do-De-O)." My uncle had written it with Bob Hargreaves. It would be the A-side of the record.

However, "Mr. Wu," on the B-side, was the hit. The record rattled and rolled along like a ragtime locomotive. George climaxed with his perfected rhythm solo—the three-over-four syncopated split stroke was a marvel. Cliff Edwards and Johnny Marvin were left behind in the dust. Even jaded band boys wondered how the simple soul worked the trick. "I don't know," said George. "It's as daft as the song." Now, under Beryl's sartorial guidance, he was wearing natty suits and ties. His heavily oiled hair shone like the black shellac on a 78 rpm disc.

Here was a well-turned-out, wasp-waisted young man of modern times playing old-fashioned music on an un-jazzy out-of-date instrument. And with lyrics that were on a level with the naughty seaside postcards you bought on the pier for a snigger—like the one depicting a hiker, eager for a refreshing beer at the pub in the far distance, who's asking the couple having it off sweatily in a ditch: "How far is 'The Old Stump Inn'?"

Mr. Wu's wobbly eye was only the start on the road of raunchy innuendo. The laundryman's life was to be charted in a series of follow-ups by writers other than Jack Cotterill (who seemed to prefer being "Cottrell" on the song credits—changed his name like so many Alleymen of that era, including my uncle, who was Jack Stevens before he became the grandiose Stanley Damerell).

The happy couple—banjulele and Beryl.
Courtesy of Michael Daly, georgeformby.org.

MEANWHILE IN ENGLAND...

Wu got married, was proclaimed the husband of the wife of Mr. Wu (ordering geishas not to "meddle with me chopstick"), changed business to become a window cleaner (his wife, in silk stockings, grew tired of his running up her ladder), aided the war effort as an air-raid warden, and finally joined the RAF.

Before Cotterill got sacked by Beryl—for making a fuss about George grabbing credit for songs he hadn't written—he contributed a successful phallic song, the first in a long line: "With My Little Ukulele in My Hand" has George playing *with* it as opposed to *on* it and recognizing his newborn baby as a boy because he has a ukulele in his hand. There would be "om bon pongs" and "no-man's land" and a "Little Stick of Blackpool Rock" (a lettered column of hard candy), as well as "Grandad's Flannelette Nightshirt" (his bride is shocked when he pulls it out on the train) before a World War II song trumps the lot with its image of a sergeant flashing an enormous weapon.

Formby's only West End musical.
Courtesy of Michael Daly, georgeformby.org.

After an exhaustive study of this canon, one's head starts to reel and everything around transmogrifies into a sexual object—the lightbulb, the tap, the hairbrush, even a picture of Robert E. Lee. Come to think of it, George has the Confederate general as a kind of pain in the ass in "Auntie Maggie's Remedy."

This one, by Eddie Latta, also introduces masturbation, abortion, and doping too, but not so you'd be upset, because George sings smilingly, chuckling in the middle of a word, and strumming to a tune that, typically, trips along with the bright-eyed innocence of a children's song. One must keep in mind that even back in the Cotterill years, George was bringing in unusual topics like necrophilia—in "I Went All Hot and Cold" he finds himself in bed with a male corpse—and none of his public was much concerned.

General society in the 1930s was still in

HITTING THE HIGH SPOTS NOW

WRITTEN AND COMPOSED BY GEORGE FORMBY, FRED E. CLIFFE AND HARRY GIFFORD

ASSOCIATED TALKING PICTURES present

GEORGE FORMBY in **"TROUBLE BREWING"**

ASSOCIATED BRITISH FILM DISTRIBUTORS
CAMPBELL, CONNELLY & Co., Ltd.
LONDON

6ᵈ NET.

a sexually repressed state, still under a cloud of latter-day Victorian prudery. Only the very rich could afford to indulge their sexual whims without getting into hot water with the authorities, and they had big cars and houses to hide in. The average bloke was forced to relieve his frustrations in sordid venues—deep in the shaking bushes and shrubs of a park, or a back-alley wall, followed by a hasty doing-up of the trouser buttons and an adjusting of the dirty raincoat.

This was the reality that lay gray and lumpy beyond the Formby limelight. He was only letting in a little sunshine, getting some safety-valve laughter. How the ladies loved him! There are period photos of Our George signing his latest 78 surrounded by admiring, giggling women.

By the mid-1930s he was Britain's best-selling recording artist, the first native pop star.

On records you could do as you pleased. If it was airplay you were after, then your good taste had to be checked at the culture gate of the British Broadcasting Corporation. This was run by a stern Scotch Calvinist called John Reith, whose mission was to broadcast the British way of life and "all that was best in every department of human knowledge, endeavor,

and achievement." He didn't care for pop music, but he realized that the common man must have some relaxation, and so he instigated a Dance Music Policy Committee to vet incoming discs. Offensive ones were slapped with a sticker: "Not to Be Broadcast." This happened to George's "With My Little Ukulele in My Hand" in 1933. Decca withdrew the record and had him make a cleaner version—it was passed for broadcast.

In 1936, his new label, Regal Zonophone, having goaded George to get fruitier and filthier, released a real winner in the field of healthy smut. "The Window Cleaner" is a voyeur's dream day—told by a Peeping Tom, who from his ladder spies ladies' nighties and what goes inside, then watches an octogenarian talkie queen undressing, and finally enjoys honeymooners getting down to business.

Naturally the BBC banned it, ordering George to clean his own windows. George replied that his appeal had always been to a family audience. Privately he asked his writers for more and smuttier. Beryl told everybody that the toffs at the BBC could "fuck off." She never minced words. Anyway the record was selling at almost 200,000 a month, so there!

This prudish schoolmaster/naughty boy relationship went on into the next war, even as minds and bodies should have been concentrating on beating the Nazi threat. In 1939, with Germany starting to bomb British cities, "With My Little Stick of Blackpool Rock" was blacklisted; in 1940, with the Blitz of London about to begin, George came out with "On the Wigan Boat Express," which had a girl getting "what for in the corridor" and a chap on the engine floor waking to find "a tender behind."

The BBC's attitude towards the Wigan upstart was summed up three years later when a manager from the BBC's Northern region wrote that: "this man is essentially vulgar and seems to be incapable of producing anything that is not objectionable." Another manager added that Formby refused to accept the corporation's standards of decency: "All artists are selfish as I well know, but George Formby is a thoroughly intractable kind of person."

Their old director-general, Sir John Reith, had always backed his men to the hilt in such matters: "If the public want to listen to him singing his disgusting little ditties, they'll have to be content to hear them in the cinemas—

not over the nation's airwaves."

George had graced the cinemas screens of the North since 1934. A very low-budget company in Manchester had starred him in *Boots! Boots!*, a ramshackle affair shot over a London garage, in which he brought back the benighted John Willie character complete with father's cut-down bowler hat and put-upon manner. Violence is everywhere what with John Willie's manhandling of women, kicking a nancy boy in the behind after partnering him in an effeminate dance, and throwing a chef out of a high window. The abrasiveness is tempered somewhat by pauses for music: in the hotel cabaret finale, Beryl tap-dances beautifully to "Mr. Wu," played as an instrumental by saturnine Harry Hudson & His Melody Men, followed by a tuxedoed and svelte George with the only slightly dirty "Sitting on the Ice in the Ice Rink." He proves himself to be a balladeer at the end with a sweet love song for romancing Beryl. "Baby," like all his other numbers, has him on a large wooden ukulele. No banjulele. Why on earth not?

The next film corrects this: *Off the Dole* is ostensibly about the Great Depression (even touching on Communism), but the vagaries of the plot soon dispense with any reference to current affairs and so, while the cameraman seems to have popped round the corner for a beer, we can watch George, all gussied up again, entertain a set of sophisticates in a Mayfair drawing room on his nicely strident banjo-uke. While the toffs sit around in rictus-smile bewilderment, Our George looks straight into the camera to address his cloth-cap and muffler congregation on the subject of having his little ukulele in his hand.

Jack Cotterill songs filled these two moneymaking films, but about this time he had his run-in with Beryl and was shown the door. In fact she slammed it in his face. She'd found a new team who could not only write risqué, but agreed to play the game—the Formby name, as cowriter, would be on all their offerings.

Harry Gifford had, as we've seen, been composing for the music halls since before World War I. He'd also cowritten "All Going Back" for George Sr. In 1934, almost in his sixties, he teamed with Fred E. Cliffe, a Liverpudlian versifier who was getting on in years too, and the team gave Formby a string of comedy songs from weird exotics like "Madame Moscovitch" and the "Hindoo Man" to "The Window Cleaner" and the erotically sticky "Blackpool Rock." They could write anything to order: a touching ballad like "Goodnight, Little Fellow, Goodnight," which George sang to a child in one of his later quality films.

The songwriters were on call to come up with material at a moment's notice when, in 1935, their benefactor was signed to Associated Talking Pictures, a big southern outfit later to become the prestigious Ealing Films. Basil Dean, the head man, had guided Lancashire lass Gracie Fields into box-office stardom and he was to do the same with Formby. Surrounding George with top-notch actors (plus a few glamour girls), technicians, and scriptwriters, the studio provided a lustrous frame from which the singing fool shone out like never before. Cameramen lit him so that his eyes, teeth, and hair radiated an otherworldly personality akin to a Technicolor cartoon. Beryl spoiled this gorgeous picture by lurking around the set like a harridan, making sure George didn't get any slurpy big kisses from his female coworkers.

Feather Your Nest (1937) gave him his most enduring and endearing song, "Leaning on a Lamp-Post." Filled with a lilting insouciance destroyed at the end by the regulation Formby uke solo, this was an outside number, not written by Gifford and Cliffe, the chain-gang pair. It was the work of Noel Gay, a gentleman with class, a veteran of smart West End musical comedies and revues. In his youth, as Reginald Armitage, he'd studied classical music at Cambridge University but been deflected by his knack for writing simple, hummable, and oh-so-English songs. The jazz style was avoided. In the year of "Lamp-Post," he was hitting with the "Lambeth Walk" musical, *Me and My Girl*; he was self-sufficient, the sole creator of his work and about to establish his own publishing company. Noel Gay (the first name was inspired by Noël Coward) was not open to shady deals. There would be no credit sharing.

Beryl threw a fit. The song was a hit, as big as Mr. Wu and the window cleaner, an instant classic as clean as the driven snow. She called him rude names, she swore revenge, she said she'd take her business elsewhere. A pity, because Noel Gay, with his connections and theatrical reputation, might have become a regular supplier of respectable special material, leading the Formbys into the rarified air of the prewar West End.

In 1940 the war started in earnest and George was into the fray with a film to lift the spirits. *Let George Do It* is his masterpiece: a uke player in a Norwegian hotel band specializing in Formby material and led by a Nazi who's broadcasting messages in code, George saves the day somehow and pokes the Führer on the conk in the process. Mass Observation, a national survey organization, reckoned this action to be one of the biggest morale boosters of the war. A print of the film, retitled *Dinky Doo*, reached Russia, playing to full houses in Moscow for almost a year. A report in the newsmagazine *Russia Today* claimed that Formby followed Stalin and Churchill as most beloved in the Soviet heart. Americans were not so entranced, mainly bemused, by the here today/gone tomorrow release of the film as *To Hell with Hitler*. Nevertheless, movie moguls took note that the *Motion Picture Herald* had Formby as No. 1 British box-office attraction for the third year in succession. He was ahead of Bing Crosby, Gary Cooper, and Errol Flynn.

He was now, with an income of $400,000 a year, at the top of his game. He was King of All Media. And now the war was to bring his "Finest Hour."

George was always at his best down among the customers as opposed to up on the screen or spinning on a record. He'd been flummoxed by a little girl fan who, upon being introduced to him, exclaimed: "You're not George Formby! George Formby is a record!"

Beryl made the Formby brand, live and in person, available for the war effort right off the bat. She collared Basil Dean, the quality film chief, at a preview of *Let George Do It* and demanded action. Dean, recently appointed head of the Entertainments National Service Association, was desperate for top entertainers who'd agree to go the battle zone and cheer up the troops. Not for nothing was ENSA soon to be known in the trade as "Every Night Something Awful." He also wanted to get the pushy and foulmouthed Beryl off his back.

So the husband-and-wife team, dressed in standard uniforms except for George's riding britches, were immediately packed off to France to entertain the beleaguered little Brit-

ish Expeditionary Force standing at ready as the Nazis raced to the coast. The Formbys were the first variety artists in and the last out. They were leading the patriot pack, shaming their colleagues back home and abroad ("Lazy sunbathers," George called them).

They worked their war with zeal and pluck—George pulling out his uke at every opportunity no matter how big or small the audience, with Beryl at his side ready to prompt, announcing the master's presence in her adopted cut-glass proper accent. They popped up everywhere:

Now out in the Middle East, uking about "Frank on His Tank" to thousands of howling lads in a sweltering shed with flies in his mouth and eyes; now in the Holy Land telling of how Mr. Wu is doing his duty as an air raid warden, enforcing the blackout by informing you that if you have chink in your window you'll soon have a Chink at your door, ha ha, hee hee; now back to Britain for stuffy concerts where the officers and their wives have reserved up-front seats but look at their watches or at the ceiling, bored by this common man, and George telling the lads he'll give them a special show out back afterwards and the colonel threatening to report his behavior to the War Office and Beryl telling him to shove it because they're civilians and, what's more, paying their way.

Now the very first entertainers into France a few days after the D-Day invasion and handing out little sticks of Blackpool Rock and singing "I'm a Froggie" in an Amiens church and how the French love it and don't mind the words; now up against a wall of sandbags or with back to a war-torn tree surrounded by squatting lads, and next minute having tea with Field Marshal Montgomery and that night, as he sits among his men, making him crack up at "Fanlight Fanny," the frowsy nightclub queen, who's "a peach but she's always canned."

Now, with Monty's blessing, making it up to the very front line—a mere one hundred yards from the enemy—and told not to mind that his soldier audience is concealed in foxholes and not to worry because once the Germans hear the familiar voice and uke they'll not let loose any firepower; now witnessing a bomb attack and the aftermath of blood and scattered body parts and wishing there were a trigger on his uke.

In 1945, when it was all over, the authorities estimated that Formby had entertained three million Allied servicemen and women. He was awarded the OBE in the King's Birthday Honors List. He was very grateful, but commented: "We weren't looking for anything of this sort, but if something was coming our way, I'd have liked it to have been something Beryl could have shared."

It would seem bizarre, at first take, to imagine Our George in alien climes proclaiming his insular class-bound songs and not only getting away with it but being adored by all nationalities and colors. At second take, I realize that the Formby library offers a varied repertoire ranging from domestic issues through exotic foreigners to the puppetry of the penis, unlike the more restricted works by the high-flying, endlessly acclaimed legends of the American Musical—Rodgers and Hart, Cole Porter, the Gershwin brothers—who deal mainly in the sole subject of variations on a love theme. As Stanley Damerell, the erstwhile Formby supplier of songs, once put it when describing the limitations of Yankee pop: "These Yank songs are no more than the lugubrious lamentations of a disappointed lover on a couch."

George was out there in the open, happy as a Wigan nightingale.

The rest of the 1940s were to be a bit of a letdown. Like Churchill, he was yesterday's hero. The last film, *George in Civvy Street* (1946), was one of a string made for Columbia Pictures and you'd think, seeing as how he'd topped the British box office, that Hollywood might have beckoned. But both Columbia and George understood that his was an insular package and would perish on opening. Americans didn't twig, and never have, and that's that.

Actually, he'd slipped in the film-star ratings at home, as had all his fellow comedians, overtaken by a straight-faced dramatic idols like James Mason, Stewart Granger, and Laurence Olivier. Never secure about his talent—he saw himself as a daft incompetent fool, nothing like as good as his father—George now had a nervous breakdown and spent over a month in a psychiatric ward. Beryl considered having him institutionalized in a "loony bin."

However, they needed to replenish the bank account—the Labour Party that had defeated Churchill and his Conservatives after the war was hell-bent on taxing the rich, and the Formbys were soon paying almost 98 percent of their earnings to the Socialists for things like free health care for the people. "The People's War" had been all very well and good, but the Formbys had a lifestyle to maintain—one thoroughly approved of by their fans: a string of fine houses, expensive cars, pleasure cruisers, and assorted dogs.

As soon as George was well, Beryl arranged for a bunch of Commonwealth tours. To do him good—singing was always his best therapy. The first was in South Africa where, as in all the old

Empire colonies, George was a favorite through films and records. Performances were segregated, of course, and at one all-black show Beryl spontaneously picked up and kissed a little girl who'd given her a box of chocolates before handing her over to George. The blacks cheered but the politicians were not amused. Dr. Malan, head of the National Party and soon to be the prime minister who made apartheid the law of the land, rang the hotel to complain. Beryl took the call and, after she'd had quite enough of his fuming, told him off in no uncertain terms with much use of four-letter words, so the story goes. It was understood that the tour must be terminated and the couple were advised to leave South Africa quickly and quietly.

George, as the keeper of a boardinghouse that included Mr. Wu, the Hindoo Man, the cannibal Zulus of "Wunga Bunga Boo," and native cabaretters "In the Congo," was in complete agreement with his wife's stance on racial equality and packed up his ukes accordingly.

In 1951, with no more films, but with variety show bookings and recordings in which he was content to toddle along reprising the old chestnuts, he got an invitation to star in what would be his first real West End musical. George was at last in the scented realm of high-class theater as a real actor with witty lines and well-made songs far from the salty air of Gifford and Cliffe.

The writers of *Zip Goes a Million* were Cambridge University graduates with a résumé of sophisticated songs: Eric Maschwitz had written the words to "A Nightingale Sang in Berkeley Square," while George Posford had scored such stylish films as *Invitation to the Waltz*. One of the songs, "Ordinary People," showed Formby as softly reflective and even philosophical.

The producer, though, was wise enough to let George be George and bring out the uke to give them one of the old 'uns in "Pleasure Cruise."

The musical played to packed houses from the start, and although the *Daily Mail* critic praised it as a "Lancashire pot-pot served on a silver salver," the *Evening Standard* man, Kenneth Tynan, after admitting that George's "piercing, sunny little singing" was a London pleasure, went on to complain: "I cannot laugh as he fidgets and gapes and fusses flat-footed across the stage . . . I am unable to accept the theory that a banality or a catch-phrase acquires wit or 'philosophy' when delivered in a North Country accent." George was devastated when Beryl read him out the review—a little close to a home truth from the snotty South.

Six months into the run he had a massive heart attack. Queen Mary sent her personal physician. He never returned to the show, which ran on for years with others trying to substitute. For the rest of the decade he took it easy but couldn't resist appearing in the odd revue and pantomime, as well as on television and radio. I audiotaped the TV shows and learned all the songs; I was thrilled and amazed that as the guest castaway on BBC's celebrated *Desert Island Discs* he picked several records that were my favorites too and which, as a twelve-year-old, I'd bought with my own pocket money: "McNamara's Band" by Bing Crosby, "Never Trust a Woman" by Phil Harris, and "The Shot Gun Boogie" by "Tennessee" Ernie Ford. All American, all quirky, all unlike his own work.

I wish I'd turned up at his dressing room—as a friend of mine had, bearing a trunk full of memorabilia about his father George Sr., which he'd found at a flea market. George invited the boy to tea but had nothing enlightening to say, only moans about the lack of parking around the theater. I wish I'd sneaked away from our family summer holiday resort and paid a visit to the Formbys on their motor yacht *Lady Beryl II* moored on the Norfolk Broads, or dropped into one of the many grand "Beryldene" houses and watched George as he tinkered with one of his countless cars and motorcycles, or helped Beryl write to fans on her husband's behalf, and then later at teatime gotten George's opinion on Elvis Presley and Buddy Holly. I suspected that, like me, he admired the real American originals and not the copycat British boys. My weekly pop paper, *Melody Maker*, had asked him to explain his own pop idol status in the old days: " I suppose I used to be what Cliff Richard is now—not very good, but what the public wants."

I caught Formby's farewell performance on BBC television in late 1960 while studying hard for entrance qualifications to Trinity College Dublin. Then Beryl died from cancer on Christmas Eve. A few months later, in March 1961, George died from another heart attack. His lady friend, a comely schoolteacher, was at his bedside. He'd shocked us all by confessing to the press that he and Beryl had not "been intimate" for years, that she was an alcoholic, that she was an atheist and had tried to make him renounce his Catholic faith.

I was still studying hard when 100,000 turned out for the funeral. The undertaker was Eddie Latta, writer of "Grandad's Flannelette Nightshirt." Mother Eliza almost collapsed and had to be held up by two of her sons. They were all very anxious to get out of the bitter cold and hear the reading of the will. Willie Waterbucket, the Formby dog, whimpered loudly as

his master was placed in the family grave, next to his father.

But George wasn't gone because he'd never stood there, live onstage, in front of me, with eyes lancing and teeth advancing, armed with endless optimism. Like the little girl who'd met him years ago said, George Formby was a *gramophone record*. And when, that winter, I entered Trinity College Dublin on a bitterly cold and wet evening, I had his records with me, carefully wrapped and ready for aid and comfort in a foreign country.

TESSIE O'SHEA

Tessie O'Shea was the spiritual sister of George Formby, but much rowdier. I first saw her, just as I first saw Formby, on a BBC television variety show in the 1950s. She ran on and burst like a bombshell into her signature tune, "Two Ton Tessie—from Tennessee," and then, with a smile as wide as George's, went into a banjo-uke solo that must have broken all world speed records—and her split strokes were as good as the master's. She was attractively overweight, and suddenly she ran offstage with the certain grace that fat women can have. Only a bullet could have stopped her.

Twenty years later we were introduced at a parking lot in Los Angeles. It was disgustingly hot, but she didn't care and her fur wrap didn't seem to bother her. She was quiet, even pensive. When I asked what had brought her so far from her Florida home, she sighed and, calling me "love," said she'd come to do her act at a music hall in Santa Monica, but the hall was closed due to earthquake problems and anyway her back was playing up like the devil.

Tessie with banjo uke.
From the collection of Michael Daly.

Tessie's signature tune.
Courtesy of the estate of Lou Handman.

"Must have been that fall from the pregnant elephant."

Despite her Lancashire accent, her "song-claim" to be from Tennessee, and her Irish name, Tessie O'Shea was in fact from Cardiff in Wales, born in 1913. The same year as my mother, just as Formby was born the same year as my father. Nice to have a connection. She was extremely precocious: at three she clambered onto a table at a garden party and proceeded to bawl out "An Egg, an 'Am, and an Onion"; at four she won first prize—a stick of rock—at a talent contest; at eight she was in a concert party; at fifteen she was appearing in Blackpool, seaside paradise of the Northern working classes, where Formby reigned supreme.

Next thing she was down in Bristol (Uncle Art Satherley's old home town) at the Hippodrome, billed as "the Un-Wee One" on account of putting on a few pounds. By this time she was featuring "I Wish I Was Thinner" and "Nobody Loves a Fat Girl." At the Chiswick Empire in tough-to-please London, she clicked at once—unlike Our George. She was always to be big down south. She was able to trim her sails and some thought she was a cockney. Lawrence Wright, the music publisher, welcomed her to his office and said he had an American number

that would be just the ticket for her rotund persona and her banjo-uke: "Two Ton Tessie" by Tin Pan Alleymen Roy Turk and Lou Handman ("Are You Lonesome Tonight?"), with authentic Hawaiian uke arrangement by M. Kalua. This Tennessee gal is four hundred pounds, but the guys keep hanging around her because she can sit six sweeties on her knee while they play tennis on her double chin.

Tessie, the Welsh one, loved it and in the summer seasons of Lawrence Wright's *On with the Show*, which he produced at the North Pier at Blackpool, she had to encore and encore it,

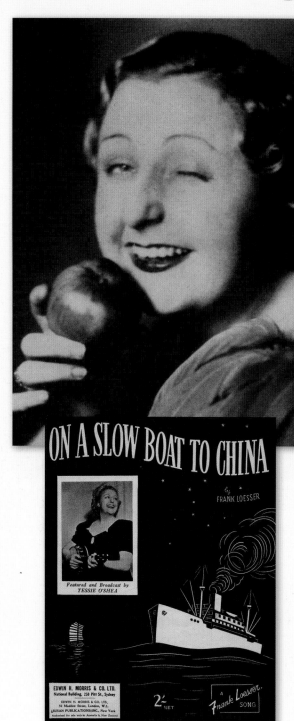

The pure gold of the music hall.
From the collection of Michael Daly.

Tessie's take on a big American hit.

each time ending with a banjo-uke solo that was right up there with Formby. She loved him and he loved her. In July 1939, two months before the war, she cut "Two Ton Tessie" for Parlophone, the same label that just over twenty years later the Beatles were signed to by George Martin.

Tessie had been recording since the early 1930s but, despite a wide range of killing stuff, she never had a hit. Today her "Nobody Loves a Fairy When She's Forty" by the comic song specialist Arthur ("What Do You Give a Nudist for His Birthday?") Le Clerq, is considered a classic; and "Live and Let Live" is a gentle lesson in universal tolerance; "You're at Blackpool by the Sea" is a travel guide to the pleasures in store, such as chomping "yards and yards of tripe—the stomach issue of a sheep or ox, best taken with fried onions.

In the war, like Formby, she pulled her weight as an ENSA act, contributing "I Fell in Love with an Airman Who Had Big Blue Eyes, but I'm Nobody's Sweetheart Now." It was in 1944 during a London revue that she made a grand stage entrance on the back of Mrs. Jumbo, the pregnant elephant, was tossed off, seriously injured, and was out of commission for three months—but back in action in time to star in front of the king and queen at the Royal Variety Show.

On the screen, she followed Formby by making films for the same Manchester studio that had started his career. She graduated to

Ealing Studios in 1950 (they had dropped Our George during the war in order to go upmarket, a little brainier, artsier) with her cameo in the film-noir neo-realist *The Blue Lamp*, playing herself onstage at the Metropolitan Theatre, Edgware Road, one of the last of the great music halls. She was boy criminal Dirk Bogarde's alibi as she sang "There Isn't Enough to Go Round" while he murdered a friendly copper in a nearby cinema.

As the music halls closed, Tessie was saved by Noël Coward, who cast her as a cockney fish-and-chips seller in his Broadway musical *The Girl Who Came to Supper*. The sophisticated and jaundiced Coward, noting her New York arrival in his diary, described her as "exuding synthetic good humour from every pore, but she is going to do the 'London' song marvellously and will probably tear the place up."

This became a lifesaver when the show opened in December 1963. President Kennedy had been just been assassinated and America was in need of a fillip. Tessie brought down the house with "London Is a Little Bit of All Right," receiving a five-minute standing ovation. Coward wrote in his diary: "I have never heard such cheering. Not unnaturally, she got all the notices.

It was truly thrilling to see that rumbustious, bouncing old-timer, after some years in limbo, come back."

As a result, she guested on *The Ed Sullivan Show* in a special British edition on the fateful night of February 9, 1964. She was as terrific as usual, but it was her bad luck to be sharing the bill with the Beatles. The kids were screaming and America was watching. Tessie was totally eclipsed. Only the Beatles cared—they'd been fans of hers (and of George Formby) since childhood.

She found more work in America as a typical cheerful cockney character. As a film actress, she won an Academy Award nomination for *The*

Glamour girl of the silver screen.
From the collection of Michael Daly.

Russians Are Coming, The Russians Are Coming in 1966. She proved herself to be a Shakespearean as the nurse in *Romeo and Juliet* at the New Orleans Civic Center. She played Mrs. Hobday in the Walt Disney picture *Bedknobs and Broomsticks*. She was supposed to be appearing at the Mayfair Music Hall in Santa Monica in the early 1970s when I met her in that parking lot. She died aged eighty-two at her home in East Lake Weir, Florida, in 1995. Unlike George Formby, she'd made a mark in America.

BILLY "UKE" SCOTT

Here, with the entrance of Billy "Uke" Scott, we have an unequal banjo-uke triumvirate—unequal because Formby was financially at the top, Tessie in the middle of the sandwich for her exuberance, and Billy at the bottom for his superior musicianship, something the public as a rule doesn't really care about.

He was born in Sunderland, in the North of England in 1923, the year that Formby bought his first banjo-uke. As a boy he was taught classical piano and learned to read and write music. This was put to use when he became pianist for music hall stars Gracie Fields and Max Miller. In the Second World War, he costarred in a strange film called *A Night of Magic*, in which he was "Reggie's Pal" and is seen, a nice-looking lad, at the piano performing a rather tuneful self-written song. Peculiarly, a three-thousand-year-old Egyptian princess keeps interrupting by coming out and going back into a mummy casket. Not a good start for a cinema career. After the war, he wrote topical stuff like the postwar lament "A Nice Prefabricated Home." None became hits.

Meanwhile he'd studied the banjo-uke after being handed one by a bandleader while singing with a 1930s swing band. "Just fake it when the jazz breaks come," said the leader. Billy was intrigued by the possibilities of the uke and, unlike Formby, wasn't content to simply strum, however nifty that strum might sound. He learned to play melodies with harmonic accompaniment and all at the same time—a peppy mini orchestra. On the popular BBC radio program *Workers' Playtime*, during the 1940s and 1950s, Billy was a regular guest, but the factory workers, although polite, preferred to sing along and jig a bit rather than to sit still and be impressed by uke virtuosity. When variety (a new word for music hall) ceased to be, Billy became an agent for a while, and after that he retired to a narrow boat.

If you type in his full name at YouTube, you'll be rewarded with a video clip—a bit dim and pokey—of Billy "Uke " Scott, at a George Formby Society convention, rendering a terrific instrumental version of "Lady of Spain," which my Uncle Stanley cowrote. The chorus tune has the same descending notes as "12th Street Rag," that other uke showpiece, but Billy rattles it off with aplomb and, for my money, this is how the uke should be employed if you're simply soloing. He was president of the Ukulele Society of Great Britain. He died in 2004.

All in our triumvirate were dear to the hearts of the British people, old or young. This affection wasn't mere nostalgia. In the early 1960s, when I was one of many struggling in electric beat groups in an attempt to challenge the American rockers by offering something a little different, I nurtured the Formby spirit and strum. So did my fellow native rockers, especially George Harrison and Paul McCartney. We knew that music-hall song and spirit was our roots music, the equivalent of American blues and country. That's one of the reasons we seemed so fresh and ebullient when eventually we invaded America.

Billy on his banjo-uke—he took to the louder uke sound when playing in dance bands.

Arthur Godfrey—the jaunty captain of the airwaves. From the collection of Flea Market Music.

CHAPTER FIVE

ARTHUR GODFREY

PAPA WITH THE PLASTIC UKE

Arthur Godfrey, ruler of the airwaves in the early 1950s, was a uke player and teacher, so he must have been a good guy. But there were others, people he worked with, who felt their boss was more fitted to the black hat. All that folksy clipping of the "G" from the end of the word—all of that was a fraud.

The homespun, people-pleasing, warm, baritone voice capable of selling any product it truly believed in—from peanut butter to Navy recruitment—could, off the air, be abusive and profane should your loyalty to the master be in doubt. Producers nodded and smiled when he told them confidential tales that they knew were lies, and then they ran to the bathroom to punch themselves in the mirror; when he asked, "How was it?" none dared tell him the show had been rotten. He was the Big Papa of the old plantation and if you bounced high and delighted him, he might make you, an unknown, into a "Little Godfrey," a regular on the daily radio show or on the evening TV shows. But you were his creature, his serf, and if you got too big for your boots, got an agent, became a star, then you were out.

He fired his boy singer Julius La Rosa for having two hit records, too much fan mail, and refusing to attend dancing lessons like all the other kids. He fired him live on the air and afterwards told the press the reason was his boy's "lack of humility." There followed some more head chopping, including his producer for daring to get engaged to one of his Little Godfrey girl singers. She got fired too. Only The Ole Redhead, as he liked to call himself, was allowed to touch them, even give them an avuncular goose.

Then there was his longtime house bandleader Archie Bleyer, a man who really should have shown allegiance after all that had been done for him. Instead the guy goes and starts a record

From the collection of Flea Market Music.

company, Cadence, and steals a raft of the beginners that he, Arthur Godfrey, had groomed and petted and let his magnanimous spotlight shine brightly upon. Take the Chordettes, small-time barbershop gals from "hicksville" Sheboygan, whom he, the Great Godfrey, had taken under his wing as long ago as 1949, when he'd invited them on to *Arthur Godfrey's Talent Scouts*. Now, here in 1954, they've been seven weeks at No. 1 with "Mister Sandman" on Cadence. Those sweet girls, who years back brought him to tears while singing that old close harmony classic "Down by the Old Mill Stream" on the TV show. And Bleyer had the nerve to marry one of them. He got the chop. What happened to good old-fashioned loyalty?

Let's continue looking at it from Godfrey's point of view. Let's bring out the big picture and go back a few decades to show how we really have a Ukulele Hero here who paid his dues.

Born in New York in 1903, raised in New Jersey, he was educated at the Varsity of Life— more than that: he didn't even complete high school. Son of an impoverished English father who pretended to an aristocratic lineage and had a series of jobs that didn't make much sense, Godfrey did the Huck Finn thing and left home at fourteen.

Next came a series of experiences as an obstacle course for eventual worldly success. A prostitute pickpocketed the ten dollars he'd made as an office boy; he took to sleeping in rolls of newsprint; he developed a hacking cough working in a coal mine; he was out of luck as a lumberjack, but he did make it for a short time in a rubber company plant before a strike closed it down and he became a dishwasher with a side job working a dice game. The Navy saved him and he sailed the world, learning to be a radio operator and a passable banjo player. A fellow seaman gave him a ukulele.

He returned to land for an intermission to study and practice the art of selling cemetery lots, followed by a little vaudeville, which ended with freight train hopping. Now the Coast Guard came to the rescue. He stayed three years, graduating in radio at the Naval Research Laboratory. It was while there that his mates, impressed by his malty voice and salty banjo songs, persuaded him to invade a local Baltimore radio station. He was hired after a few numbers. Next week he was "Red Godfrey, the Warbling Banjoist" on his own sponsored show. But it was his firm and clear enunciating with the affected British accent, inherited from his father, which impressed management. Drop the banjo, they said, and become an announcer. Soon he'd graduated to NBC in Washington.

An epiphany after a car accident pointed him in a revolutionary direction. Listening to his colleagues on the radio from his hospital bed, he realized how patronizing and stiff they all sounded. And how phony his upper-class limey voice must have sounded too. All that pompous, self-important, talking down to a distant unknown audience, as if radiomen were in a lofty ether pantheon.

He returned to NBC as a born-again; he pulled close to the mike to confide and share natural small talk with the lonely folk out there, making his studio their front parlor. He belched on air, he blew his nose; he gave uke lessons. He was on so early in the morning, nobody in management was up to hear him. One day he smashed the seven a.m. record of "William Tell" with the easy reasoning: "Ain't that the silliest thing you ever heard of?" Listeners were captivated. This was abnormal in radio but normal

in their lives: the storytelling uncle who almost went too far.

He went too far for NBC, when he kept mocking the ad copy he had to read. They fired him—and CBS was happy to take him on. Walter Winchell, the all-powerful journalist whose gossip column was read by everybody including the president, discovered the simple joys of Godfrey early one morning and telephoned from his table at the Stork Club. Next day, the newspaper plugs started coming and didn't stop. From now on, Godfrey was free to relax into the persona that radio comedian Fred Allen called "the man with the barefoot voice," echoing an innocent mythic America of back-porch philosophy, homemade meat loaf, and—who else but?—Huckleberry Finn.

He was tops at selling product his own way. He had to believe in it, whether it was Chesterfield Cigarettes or Lipton Tea and then that gave him the right to make fun of it. Describing a shampoo containing eggs and milk he said, "Why, if your hair is clean you can always use the stuff to make an omelet." He examined a steaming bowl of chicken noodle soup and declared, "I see lots of noodles. I do not see any chicken." He tasted it: "Yes, that is chicken. It might have walked through the water once." Copywriters tore their hair; listeners bought the soup in bulk.

This T.V. Pal uke was manufactured by Mario Maccaferri as a lower-cost cousin of the Islander series. An endorsement from Arthur Godfrey fell through, however the partial face on the head-stock does resemble Godfrey somewhat.
From the collection of Flea Market Music.

Sincerely Yours
Arthur Godfrey

From the collection of Flea Market Music.

By this time, the late 1940s, he was a household name. He commanded nine sponsored radio and TV programs a week. Technology was made human: "Ha-whya, ha-whya, ha-whya!" was his beloved greeting to the faithful millions all over the land. For being himself, he was making the CBS network ten million dollars a year, accounting for 12 percent of their ad revenue. God was short for Godfrey, said the wags. His producers might have had other words—they never knew what he was going to do next. "If I say what comes to my mind first, that's usually the best thing . . . I don't like to think too much about something. Just as soon as I start figuring it out, I get loused up."

He was acting on an impulse and an instinct based on genuine love and devotion when in January 1950 he started promoting the ukulele. He'd always had a place in his heart for the old songs and now he was pushing an old favorite—ukulele, which had been put into a rest home by the bulldozer riffs of the big swing bands. But the bands had faded and pop music was in hiatus. Novelty filled the gap: Godfrey had already enjoyed a clutch of hit records including "Too Fat Polka (I Don't Want Her, You Can Have Her, She's Too Fat for Me)" and "Slap 'Er Down Again, Paw."

For six solid months, on both his radio and TV shows, dressed in a Hawaiian shirt, he strummed and sang easy pop on a specially designed baritone uke. He was pretty good and his whimsical Pickwickian vocal style was winning. He gave lectures on the merits of the uke; he gave lessons twice a week on Tuesdays and Thursdays. He spoke out against dud ukes, telling *The Billboard*, the trade paper: "I have been cautioning my listeners against throwing away money on cheap, poorly made instruments no-

body can play. And since a couple of the fakers have threatened suit, which I would welcome, I think I must have done some good." More good was hoped for in his message to parents: "If a kid has a uke in his hand, he's not going to get into much trouble."

The result was astounding and a shot in the arm for the stagnant uke business. Average annual sales of a few thousand shot up to that many sales a week after Godfrey got proselytizing. This was the first Great Ukulele Revival. He received a ukulele embossed with a signed letter from the Governor of Illinois:

You have made Chicago and Illinois UKE-CONSCIOUS! We salute you through the Herald-American, *which is distributing thousands of ukuleles to its subscribers. Our police tell us that boys and girls who make music keep out of mischief . . .*
Cordially,
Adlai E. Stevenson.

Godfrey's baritone uke, sounding more like a sawn-off guitar, was an expensive instrument. One day, on a pile of product ranging from floor wax to flour and longing to be endorsed, he picked up a soprano uke called "The Islander" made by Maccaferri of the Bronx, a branch of the French-American Reed Co. Must be a toy, the kind of thing that gets the uke a bad name, that prevents the Musicians Union from recognizing us. He strummed. It was fine. Such sweet sounds from a piece of plastic. On the air he endorsed it—without payment:

"I'll tell you what's available—and I've been looking for it for a long time, so that the average person would be willing to buy it. That's this ISLANDER, a plastic ukulele . . . . It frets good, has good tone! Mathematically it's perfect and you can play on it. See—a good tune and it's only $5.95!"

Mario Maccaferri was flabbergasted when within days of Godfrey's announcement and demonstration, his factory was inundated with orders for the Islander. Soon his workers were managing to turn out twenty-four hundred a day, but orders were backed up—the goal was to step up production to six thousand of these babies a day. Jack O'Brian, a onetime Godfrey adversary, reported for the *New York Journal-American* on August 20, 1950:

A year ago the plant employed fewer than 110 persons. As of today, more than 250 lads and lasses are hard at it, shaping in plastic the musical futures of a great many back porch, sandy beach and mountain resort romances.

Indeed America had gone uke-crazy and this was so right for an era intent on forgetting the strictures and horrors of the past war or any war, in order to concentrate on making life in a safe home agreeable, untaxed by any pesky outside reality. Would the uke become a permanent household fixture like the piano used to be? May Singhi Breen had written in her *New Ukulele Method*, capitalizing on the craze, that "thanks to the one and only Arthur Godfrey, the ukulele is now called 'the family instrument of America.'"

A great man with vision and power, Godfrey, like John Wesley in the Great Awakening, had roused the people from their torpor, got them up from off their couches and recliners, started them plinking and plunking. In October, the New York branch of the Musicians Union, the toughest of the bunch, finally gave in—mainly due to May Singhi Breen's lengthy campaign—and let uke players go pro. But did the movement have staying power?

Alas, next year uke sales slipped 50 percent and remained low, going down and down till by the mid-sixties they were almost zero.

Where had the new ukesters gone? Home to watch TV and catch Lawrence Welk playing uke, or that nice Pat Boone and the even nicer and cutely exotic Poncie Ponce, the native detective in *Hawaiian Eye*. Let the professionals entertain us as we munch and slouch! The people had put away their ukes till the lazy, crazy days of summer. A fun thing, a pleasantry. Of no importance.

But King Arthur had tried his best. A genuine missionary. He even went so far as to try and hook his millions onto jazz, an all-American invention the majority had never really taken to in its pure form. *Jazz for the People* he called the 1960 LP and he enlisted some solid senders, led by Dick Hyman, to lie on top of his baritone uke as he crooned through Alley and Broadway standards. It was a truly eclectic mash, ringleadered by an enthusiastic Godfrey announcing each soloist throatily and happily letting him jazz up the hallowed old favorites.

He expressed his newfound discovery of jazz quite well on the back of the LP:

"Maybe I'd been listening to too much 'wall-to-wall' music, that 'schmaltzy' sound that's played by a Hundred Strings . . . Maybe on another day I had heard too much 'Rock 'n' Roll' with its deadly sameness, its heavy, electronic fish beat, its built-in urge to conformity and its terrible lack of health and humor—But suddenly Jazz became a friend, a good-humored friend that takes an old, tired melody, a somber, sententious tune from a long-deceased show and makes it into a new fresh titillating masterpiece of musical invention.

His heartfelt evangelism fell on deaf ears. The LP was not a big seller. The adult people

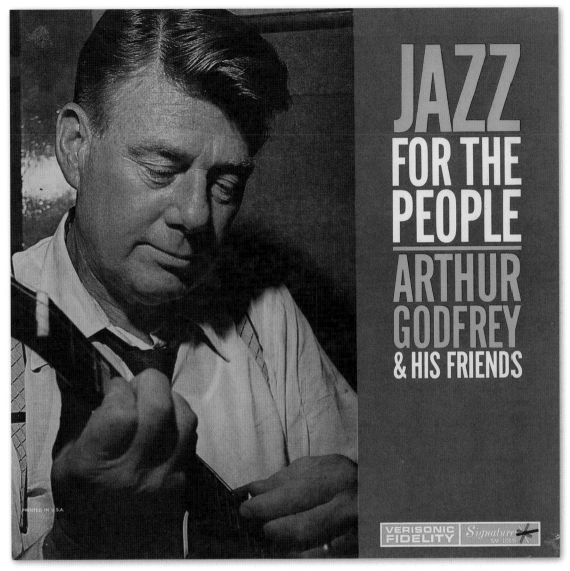

From the collection of Flea Market Music.

wanted what they'd always wanted—melody and rhythm, straight. The junior people wanted rock 'n' roll. Jazz went back to slither about in the underground of dark shades and reefers. And the ukulele appeared to have vanished from the scene. But no!

A key ingredient in recordings by Guy Mitchell, Connie Francis, and other pop stars of the 1950s is the almost-concealed ukulele.

Smuggled in and snuggling in a bed of three guitars, it provides a merry edge to such hits as Mitchell's "Singing the Blues" and Francis's "Everybody's Somebody's Fool." George Harrison could hear the little imp, and so could John and Paul. And so could I.

ARTHUR GODFREY

CHAPTER SIX

IAN'S STORY

THE GOLDEN AGE HAS ENDED
(NOT FORGETTING TINY TIM)

"I'm not going to work down the mine"—or words to that effect—says a doltish character repeatedly to a recruiting officer in *Somewhere on Leave*, one of the service farces made in the war by Mancunian, the Northern England film company that produced the first George Formby vehicles.

As an aspiring music hall performer at eighteen, I ought to have gone down into the mines myself or worked in a cotton mill or heaved bricks on a building site. Or done something manual, sweating and swearing, coughing and spitting, wearing a work jacket, driven by a determination to spit the grit and clamber up to stardom sporting the badge of impeccable street cred.

But it couldn't be.

I loved the people's songs and had, borrowing my cousin's toy uke, mastered the rudimentary positions that let me perform "Mr. Wu's a Window Cleaner" and "Your Baby Has Gone Down the Plughole." My show, however amusing to relatives and school friends, was a million cultural miles from the working-class roots.

You see, I was upper middle class—anybody "common" could immediately spot that from my expensive accent taught to me at exclusive boarding schools. And I ought to have been imitating Noël Coward if I wanted to be true to my class or, with less integrity, be head-down and hard-studying blues, folk, or jazz like my school pals were doing.

They'd raise themselves, temporarily casting aside cricket caps and rugger shirts, to put jazz horns to their rose petal lips and hunch their Rupert Brookeian bodies in slavish imitation of Buddy Bolden or Satchmo, lavishing "Yeagh!" and "Go, man, go!" on each other. When an apple-cheeked trumpeter smeared a note so blue it blushed, or the singer—top boy in economics and modern European history, now calling himself "Bubber Joe" or "One Legged Pete"—growled impressively about a life in the Delta with corn whiskey and yellow women and pumping away all night long—I knew this to be false.

What I wanted was a music hall, but they were all closing.

I left Bryanston, my school set in the lush southwest English countryside, in 1959, the year George Formby played Yarmouth Pier and I'd missed him. I left in a blaze of glory so far as the younger boys were concerned, for although I'd had doubts about pretending to be a black jazzman, I did lead a rock 'n' roll trio at an ad hoc concert in the big schoolroom at the end of the summer term. So I wasn't being truly true to my British roots. I knew three guitar chords and I slashed at them mercilessly, letting the distortion crash about in desecration of the room where Keats and Shelley were normally taught. I did sing a local number, "High Class Baby," a current hit by England's own Cliff Richard, plus some early Elvis. The junior boys cheered; the older jazz aficionado boys grimaced. My housemaster put his pipe in his pocket and stalked out. The English literature master, an aesthetic bachelor, gave me the nod and invited me to discuss Elvis et al at a later date.

All my life I'd loved pop songs and had sung them at every opportunity, encouraged by wonderful parents who catered to my every whim. My father played classical piano beautifully, but had trouble with syncopation and asked me for tips. My grandfather, an oil millionaire, frequented the music halls in his Edwardian youth and liked to sing me the choicer ones complete with gestures. His sister had married downmarket—to Stanley Damerell, a cockney who, as you know, cowrote several of the early George Formby numbers as well as hits like "Lady of Spain" and "Let's All Sing Like the Birdies Sing."

Uncle Stanley was elected King Rat, head of the Grand Order of Water Rats, the variety performers' benevolent society, and invited the family to their functions. The Rats were an eccentric lot, greeting each other with a ritual dropping of false teeth followed by the passing of a midget comedian, "Wee" Georgie Wood, from lap to lap along the dinner table. My grandfather got to sing "I'm Henery the Eighth, I Am" as a duet with its performer Harry Champion. All this became family lore from which I was later to benefit.

Ian's Uncle Stanley Damerell in the guise of King Rat accepting a cigarette from Sir Malcolm Campbell with "Wee" Georgie Wood hovering behind.

During the war, up in Scarborough where my RAF father was stationed, I'd piped "All the Nice Girls Love a Sailor" a cappella while on the chamber pot. At prep school I'd formed a lavatory (tissue) paper and comb band. I banged out music hall songs on the school piano at Bryanston until they banned all pop and even jazz as interfering with academic studies. This made me want to play pop even more because it was out of bounds. Teachers had for years, and from school to school, tried to instruct me in proper piano, to read and play scales and Chopin. But I wanted to perform immediately, to force the notes out my way, to make up my own songs. You could get instant music from a keyboard—the same with my cousin's ukulele. French horn and trumpet took years of study; I know because I tried. "Your lip's gone, son," said Mr. Hindmarch. "Let's have a smoke." Once, when I tapped my foot to an étude, Miss Wilson, my piano teacher, stepped on my foot and snapped: "Don't ever do such a thing! That's what common or dance band pianists do!" The end-of-term music report for spring 1958 stated:

"Could be taught to play quite well if he were prepared to practice—but as he says he has no intention of doing this, the decision to stop piano lessons is a very wise one."

So here I was in late 1959 with no plans for a career in music, but with a boy's head full of febrile ideas for sudden fame via the arts. First it was painting: useless—no words, no movement. Then it was becoming a film director in the footsteps of the great Russian silent directors: we had a close family friend, John Bryan, who'd won an Academy Award for his art direction of David Lean's *Great Expectations*. And now, here he was offering me a job as fifth assistant director on the upcoming *Tunes of Glory* at Shepperton Studios to be directed by his colleague Ronald Neame and starring Alec Guinness and John Mills. What a chance! From assistant director, I could go to the cutting room and from there to directing. Of course, this would all take years. You must work your way up step by step in the business; you must learn to be part of a team.

Needless to say, I was no bloody good. My job was to make the tea, crank out the script pages for the next day's scenes, call cabs for the actors, and so forth. I argued about the merits of George Formby with an old film worker who much preferred the father. I played my Eddie Cochran records. I spilled tea on the director's suit. I tried to suggest how the film should end. On the set I was a nuisance, talking loudly about the editing technique of Pudovkin or the Odessa Steps sequence of Eisenstein. In the end, the daily shooting went like this: First assistant director (shouting): "Lights! Camera! Quiet on the set! And shut up, Ian!"

Clearly, being behind the camera was not for me. So, after a little analysis of my emotions and instincts—which is how I operate—I decided that a retreat into boyhood would be best: I would return to the closeted world of school. And as I was fast becoming an adult, the only way to do this would be to become a university student. Oxford and Cambridge were closed shops for me academically. So I opted for an eccentric old-world place far away in Ireland—Trinity College Dublin, an institution still stuck in the eighteenth century, ruled by priests, soaked in whiskey and stout, and easy to enter. There resided, and had done for years, undergraduate Egyptian princes, African lords, minor Scottish aristocrats, as well as ordinary students studying the art of brewing and the making of marzipan, et cetera.

I qualified with ease and in 1961 enrolled as an undergraduate in modern history (from the fall of the Roman Empire to the start of the Great War). There was little work, few lectures, and much study off campus, especially in bars. As our barman skillfully sliced the excess foam from off the top of a freshly pulled Guinness, our history instructor, whose face grew dangerously more rubicund with every class, discussed medieval Spain, advising us that we could do no better than to see *El Cid*, which was currently playing in O'Connell Street at the cinema once managed by James Joyce. It was that kind of university. And I enjoyed the loose schedule because it gave me plenty of time off to pursue my kind of music.

Almost immediately I'd joined the college jazz band as pianist and vocalist and whatever other positions had become open. There was great attrition in membership due to drink and women. The band was a cooperative living above a fried-food café in the same unmade bed. They were good souls at heart but an odd and contentious bunch: many were the times the trombonist wrapped his horn around the head of the clarinetist during an argument about a certain classic 1920s blues; the banjoist, who had lost his strumming hand years ago in an industrial accident, played with the pick stuck into the stump and in fast numbers was seen to bleed. Many a gig ended up in fisticuffs and so I soon grew tired of this kind of jazz.

Besides, by this time I'd been introduced to a newer and more exciting beat—rhythm and blues. An Old Etonian played me import records of James Brown and His Famous Flames, with his hoarse orders to get down and get on with the good times, of Muddy Waters and his erotic boasts about being your hoochie coochie man, of Willie Dixon and his positive statement that, although tubby, he was built for comfort not for speed. They were all American, they were all splendidly black, not pale-faced, red-faced white, and therefore they were all authentic, their records taking me on a Technicolor travelogue into a place far from the dirty rain and bitter cold of Dublin.

I started a group called Warren Whitcomb & His Bluesmen. I tried hard, till my vocal cords were in shreds, to sound like a black man who had been down in the bottom but was rising to the top. I neglected my George Formby LPs.

Then in the summer of 1963 I made my first trip to America, a trip I'd dreamed about for years. I fully intended to kiss the tarmac on arrival, for I was at last visiting the source of the Big Beat, the crucible of molten rhythm where everyone must be hopping and jumping and speaking in tongues riddled with rough-hewn rocking rhyme.

But the first impression I got, as we Union of Students of Ireland were being processed into the land of the free, was of men and women in uniform, of a polite conformity, of a certain Germany. This impression continued as I journeyed through the States on a Greyhound bus. It was "Sir" this and "Sir" that and please obey the rules, sir. However, unlike my fellow students who deserted to see set sights like Washington and the Grand Canyon, I was hellbent on seeing Nashville and New Orleans, my music centers: I stepped onstage at the Grand Ole Opry and shook the hand of a startled Hank Snow; I sat in on piano with a jazz band at Preservation Hall. And in Los Angeles, killing time in the dreary downtown while waiting for a hosting family friend, I saw a ukulele in a pawnshop window and, on impulse, bought it for twenty-five dollars' worth of travelers checks. It was an old Martin soprano and so I had the finest brand straight off.

It's really not very hard to get reasonably acceptable music from the uke. I'm left-handed but, as up to this point I'd never owned a uke, I'd never bothered to restring a borrowed instrument. I learned the chords upside down and some of them I had to form from scratch. Old sheet music showed the finger positions as grids and my basic rhythm stroke was made with the first finger supported by the thumb. To produce a serviceable accompaniment was easy and effective. Some of the magic lay in the way the strummed chords followed each other naturally, as if born to do so, providing a brick pathway on which the melody, like a dancing butterfly, might gambol.

I loved the honest little uke for its stripping of harmony down to the bare essentials so that an overdressed dandy was now naked except for shorts, shirt, and shoes. Chords with hellishly complicated names—flatted nine with a raised fourth—were really just members of the same decent family, posing as exotic artist types in beard and beret.

The final trick, once the rudest technique had been mastered, lay in exuding, or even radiating, a distinctive personality as you performed. That was what I had been doing reasonably well, dog-like all of my life. As my mother liked to tell me in total kindness: "If it wasn't for your stutter, you'd be impossible—nothing stops the stream of song and chatter. You're a veritable singing magpie!"

From Los Angeles I bused to Seattle to visit a cousin. On arrival she suggested we drop into a coffeehouse down at Pioneer Square in the old skid row area. College pals of hers ran the joint—and seeing a stage I dashed up and sang a few music hall songs, showing off the Martin. I was hired straight away—the pay was free pizza and a bed—and so for the rest of that fateful summer of 1963, I entertained as a quaint limey. "The Window Cleaner" was always good for a laugh, and for variety's sake I'd sit at the upright piano and knock off "Great Balls of Fire," much to the annoyance of the purist and puritanical folkies who seemed to infest such coffeehouses at this time.

The piano restricted my field of action, like a general stuck behind a desk while trying to attack the enemy. The uke liberated me, allowing a run around the club, working the kids with grimaces and swagger and comments.

I discovered fast that American girls were fascinated by my accent. Britain was to them, in those pre-Beatle days, a strange country populated by men with bowler hats and umbrellas, where everything stopped for tea. After hours, in some secluded spot I'd work my charm on a squeaky clean girl. "You were meant for me," I'd sing, with the Martin as accomplice, and she'd ask: "D'ya really mean that?" Such venerable Alley songs could be dangerous.

Next year I was invited back to the coffeehouse and to a changed America. President Kennedy had been assassinated, the Beatles had conquered, and the Rolling Stones were coming. The sign above the door announced: "Ian Whitcomb—Direct From London Via Liverpool!"

During the year I had founded a group called Bluesville, Dublin's first R&B outfit. We were initially dedicated to playing strictly from the true black blues repertoire, but gradually I diluted the brew with current pop and even started writing special material. You see, I had

discovered that not only did American girls find me attractive but also Dublin ones. It was only the stuck-up English girls from my own class who had no time for me.

Bluesville became the hottest beat band in the Republic, rivaled only by Them (with Van Morrison) in Ulster. I threw myself around onstage in the Jagger manner. I jumped on the piano, or out into the audience. I knew I had made it when a letter arrived in the mailbox of my college rooms:

Ian, I would like to have intercoarse [sic] with you at your earliest convenience. Yours, Moira

Over in America that summer, I got myself a record contract with a Seattle label called

Ian in action with his group, Bluesville.

Jerden. I had presented the owner with a crinkled tape of a Bluesville R&B instrumental, telling him I was about to be as big as Mick Jagger. I even resembled him. The label owner made an O with thumb and first finger. Thrilled to be a potential future rock 'n' roll star, I returned to the student cellar and continued with the uke songs. One of the more amusing ones I'd discovered on an LP by one Max Morath, a ragtime revivalist in straw hat and garters: "Where Did Robinson Crusoe Go with Friday on Saturday Night?", an Al Jolson hit from 1916. I put it aside for future use because now my sights were set on creating a hit record.

That story is told in detail in two other books of mine, *After the Ball* and *Rock Odyssey*, both available from the publisher of the very book you're reading. Suffice it to say that in early 1965, while still a TCD undergraduate, Bluesville and I, in a fit of absence of mind like the men who founded the British Empire, recorded a thing with no set name, an orgasmic panting novelty with words made up as we rolled along, punctuated at the climax by a phrase I'd learned the summer before from a Seattle girl with whom I'd been sitting, lying, cuddling one night as she whispered breathily, "Ian, your accent is really turning me on."

What a striking image! You turn on a tap, a TV, an electric kettle, but not love. The unknown girl's expression became "You Turn Me On," which by July had raced up as high as No. 8 on the Billboard Hot 100, topped by Herman's Hermits and the Rolling Stones. I had achieved my goal. I was now safely a teen

Ian recording a follow up to "You Turn Me On" at Annex Studio in Hollywood, 1965.
Photo by George Sherlock.

idol. The little girls screamed, tore at my clothes and hair, did all the right things. I was on the cover of 16 magazine; I was closing act on the TV show *Shindig*; I played the Hollywood Bowl; Mick Jagger quizzed me backstage, William Burroughs wrote to my record; Paul McCartney worked in his bookshop with me as easy listening, Andy Warhol was intrigued, and Mae West covered me. But none of this ensured me a rock future. I was a one-hit wonder. The record was impossible to follow up.

So I followed my rapture.

At the end of a rock recording session in

Recording "Where Did Robinson Crusoe Go . . ."
in late 1965, also at Annex Studio, Hollywood.
Photo by George Sherlock.

late 1965, I slipped in "Robinson Crusoe." It was over in a trice. The Martin, which I now called "Ukie," dominated the guitar of the great James Burton and was supported by the beefy sax of the equally great Jim Horn. It was a jaunty affair and all over in under two minutes. Having captured the ear of America with my first novelty, I was now determined to reintroduce the ukulele to the Hit Parade. The recording engineer and owner of the studio, Thorne Nogar, loved what he heard. "A return to real music," he opined. This was the man who had recorded Spike Jones, Frank Sinatra, and Elvis Presley.

My record label, Tower, a subsidiary of Capitol, was not certain that the uke's return had commercial value. Tower Records had been started as a reaction to Capitol's initial rejection of the Beatles and other British Invaders. They didn't want to have egg on their faces again, so Tower, housed in the Capitol building, was there to release any oddball records that might float in. If the release flopped, then the headmaster didn't get the blame. If it succeeded, then Capitol took in all the money.

Tower sat on "Crusoe" for a while. I continued to make rock records but my heart wasn't in it. The drug culture was readying to swirl and envelop and I wasn't keen. I always needed to be in control of my feelings. God knows they were wild enough as it was, always running back into the past, always yearning for the missed acts at the end of the pier, for the songs my grandfather sang, for a misty landscape pierced by silv'ry moons and you in a canoe and our heads and hearts in close harmony. And Ukulele Ike describing how he's "Halfway to Heaven" as he opens the cottage gate to enter a garden where butterflies are flirting and then he spies behind a kitchen curtain his wifey cooking while she's

looking out of the window to hear that old refrain he's whistling.

What a picture! I was living in another world—had done for years—brought to me by having my head close to the comforting felt of the gramophone speaker and imagining myself clambering inside like a time traveler, adventuring down to the fundament, creeping in on the little men at work in their cave as they tooted and plucked out, like gold miners, the grand music that at any time of day or night was ready at my bidding.

I tried telling my rapture to Tower executives, but while polite, as Americans invariably are, their minds were on matters like whether to take a chance on this strange band from England called Pink Floyd or, nearer home, this one called the Standells.

One man, though, *was* listening.

George Sherlock was Tower's promotion man. It had been he who, hearing an acetate of "You Turn Me On" through the walls of the A&R office, had rushed in to proclaim: "That's a stone fox smash if I ever heard one!" They'd given him two weeks to run with the acetate and see if he could make "the mother" click at outlying radio stations. He succeeded. As a newly arrived star in Hollywood, I had been taken under his wing—letting me stay in his apartment, pulling up my collar, presenting me with deodorant spray cans, telling me to wear velour, encouraging me to eat wheat germ and drink fruit juice, and fixing me up with go-go dancers. A striking figure with his briar pipe, Dixie accent, and white hair that only grew at the back of his head but was combed in wisps to the front and teasepiled, he was proud of his notoriety as "The Under Assistant West Coast Promotion Man," flip side of the Rolling Stones' "Satisfaction."

"It's definitely a record!" said George about "Crusoe," with a boogaloo movement of his hips to emphasize his point. "But you gotta wait for the wheel of fortune to click at just the right time."

I had to wait a year, returning to my mother's home in London, playing Paris with the Stones, bus touring the Deep South with fellow Invaders. Always I had Ukie with me. Rockers were amused—particularly the Turtles—and encouraged me to get Ukie released on record.

In the summer of 1966, my chance came. For some reason there was a sudden craze for old-time music. Peter and Gordon hit with "Lady Godiva," the New Vaudeville Band reached No. 1 with "Winchester Cathedral"; there were other groups like Sopwith Camel, making a 1920s-jug band-Alley-vo-do-de-o sound. Tower joined the fray, releasing "Crusoe," and so George and I perambulated around the circle of stations surrounding Los Angeles pressing the program directors to spin us, wining and dining them and more, until, after a few weeks, my uke-soaked record was up there on the charts competing with the Beach Boys, Neil Diamond, and the Supremes. L.A. gave in and soon we were in the West Coast Top 20. The *KRLA Beat*, a reliable paper, published a nice photo of me as a "Mod-Mod" in suit and tie and deerstalker in an article headlined "Grandma's Vaudeville Sound Starts Pop Music Trend":

With the spotlight on Mod, which in turn emphasizes the intricate designs and jewelry of Yesterday, Vaudeville music could be the only follow-up to paisley, kaleidoscopes and boutiques . . . Musicians of bags other than the Good Time have a tendency to classify the Vaudeville influence as just another put-on similar to "They're Coming to Take Me Away, Ha-Haaa!"

What a mixed-up era! Nobody seemed interested in authenticity, in history—it was all fads and fashions. "I was Lord Kitchener's Batman," said a new record. Rockers wore a Regency jacket with a WWI helmet and Elizabethan pantaloons. The real past was a big joke; it was "camp," so impossibly out of date it became terribly funny. This was the arrogant sixties and anything before that was another country, another language, another piece of junk for the pot pipe.

So the vaudeville craze was only a craze, fading fast as psychedelia descended like a mushroom cloud. My peers made no sense to me. I found it increasingly impossible to follow the meandering lines in their dissertations on Life, the Universe, the Whiter Shades of Pale. My go-go dancer girlfriend named me "Eloi" and said I was an alien from a distant planet. Dr Pepper would soon be eaten up by Sgt. Pepper. I tried to play the game by covering a Beatles song as a uke vehicle: my "You Won't See Me" was allowed on Dick Clark's *Where the Action Is*

TV show, shot on Malibu Beach. I wore a muscle shirt and strummed Ukie to the kids; waiting to follow me were Captain Beefheart and a motley crew of groups in caps and makeup and with attitudes that bewildered me.

But at least I was granted time onstage at the world-famous center of folk music, the Troubadour on the western edge of Hollywood. In September of 1966, I presented my ukulele music-hall and ragtime show there for a week or so. Owner Doug Weston had warned me he was taking a chance since his club had hitherto been a temple of serious and even sententious folk music, and I was only famous for novelty rock with the uke as a latecomer. How could his

On Malibu Beach filming
Where the Action Is.

people be certain I had genuinely converted? There might be boos. Instead there were applause and laughter as, after having dismissed my rocking teenage backing band, I launched into "A Lemon in the Garden of Love" and "I'm Certainly Living the Ragtime Life," surefire Alley oldies I'd learned from my mentor "Ragtime" Bob Darch (he of the dozen martinis before the fall from the piano stool) at saloon stop-offs on the road.

My new publicist Derek Taylor, an erstwhile Beatles hand and right-hand man to Brian Epstein, brought parties night after night and joined in the choruses of World War II classics such as "We'll Meet Again"; Roger "King of the Road" Miller grabbed the mike and sang some scat about Will Rogers; Christopher Isherwood came with David Hockney. I was in seventh heaven. My stutter was the only thing preventing an explosion of excitement as introductions were made by Doug Weston. He wanted to sign me up, but I was already committed to the William Morris Agency, not forgetting a manager, road manager, publicist, music publisher, and record producer. Oh, it was all happening.

The *Los Angeles Times* reported that I was "quite good" on both ukulele and kazoo and that all in all I was "Fantastic!" Around Laurel Canyon and places where the hippies hung out, the word was to get stoned and trip out at the Troub to "Where Did Robinson Crusoe Go with Friday on Saturday Night?" The answer to that question defeated many a head.

A few months later, in February 1967, after the thrill had gone and the in-crowd had moved on to the next sensation, Derek Taylor wrote about me knowingly and with kindness in *Song Hits* magazine:

Play him a wheezing 78 of "Got A Date with an Angel" and he will sigh in deepest delight. Tell him your uncle knew a man who used to know Jolson's brother's tailor and he will be aglow with interest . . . . The really great thing about Whitcomb is that he's a genuine original. There is no one else on the scene who is either capable of, or interested in, bringing the very old to a very new environment and making the two blend.

I was all set to conquer and teach and entertain—me and Ukie alone would bring the Truth to an anxious world.

Alas, my mission was soon to encounter a roadblock: Tiny Tim.

TINY TIM

God Bless Tiny Tim was the title of his hit LP on the Reprise label in 1968, a year I remember for the slings and arrows I suffered. His success was a hindrance to my ukulele and me, and to all the world's ukuleles! For attached to his hand, as it was even on the night he married Miss Vicky on *The Tonight Show*, watched in bemusement by host Johnny Carson and forty million others (many in anger), the proud instrument that had made so much cultural progress was now, by association, a laughingstock.

Tim was no rock-star beauty—in comparison, Mick Jagger was Greta Garbo. A nose bigger than Fagin's, dank shoulder-length hair, pear-shaped body, voice like a spinster aunt one minute and a melodrama villain the next, and a uke technique limited to three chords in one key, frequently not in tune. He was used to be being yelled at as a freak and a weirdo—he blew kisses in response. On an English tour, a man took a swipe; *Newsweek* labeled him "the most bizarre entertainer this side of Barnum & Bailey's sideshow"; and a writer in the *Hartford Courant* (Connecticut) pointed out: "There is certainly some-

The hit album from 1968.

From the collection of Flea market Music.

thing wrong with this country's sense of values when teachers all over the country have to strike for decent wages and working conditions, but a no-talent freak like Tiny Tim can command $50,000 a week for his performances."

For his Warhol fifteen minutes of fame—just over a year in fact—the ukulele *was* Tiny Tim and Tiny Tim *was* the ukulele. There was nobody else competing. I wasn't in the game; I was told I was a copycat and a loser. I hid Ukie for a while.

But God bless Tiny Tim, I now say.

He must have been very difficult to live with or even to be around with—in the normal fashion. But he wasn't normal, he was extraordinary; he was brilliant in his way—I mean musicologically. Offstage there were problems.

He took up to five hour-long showers a day, even after a purely lavatorial call. No one else could use that bathroom. Then he'd climb back into dirty malodorous clothes, which, as a gesture to society, he doused with perfume. He was addicted to cosmetics, applying face cream so thickly he looked like a living statue of Pierrot. He ate alone, but sometimes entertained a half dozen phantom dinner guests, working the table, sampling each plate, chatting in voices he liked to believe were those of long-dead stars of cylinder and 78 rpm records from the turn of the twentieth century up until the early 1930s.

He was deeply religious, had taken Jesus Christ as his savior, and was convinced his life bore witness to a constant battle between the forces of good and evil. Frequently caught in the middle or tempted by s-e-x (as he called it), his talisman was a cry of "Thankgodtochrist!"

Aside from all of the above—except the old record stars—Tiny Tim and I had a lot in common. We played the same brands of ukulele—Martin, Favilla, and metal resonator Johnson—and we played left-handed without restringing. Our hearts were in Tin Pan Alley, where lived the belters and crooners of the golden age when melodies were beautiful, beguiling, haunting, with lyrics that told of girls who ought never have left home and men who swore undying love and kept their vows. In a trendy word of the times—we were soulmates.

A year or so before he died, Tiny Tim was interviewed by a journalist friend of mine. The subject of "She's a New Kind of Old-Fashioned Girl" came up. This is a morality piece, with a terrific recitation in the middle, recorded in 1929 by "Whispering" Jack Smith, a crooner who comes to me often in dreams. I recorded my version in the early 1970s and performed it on public television. "Do you do this song?" asked the journalist. "No, no!" cried Tiny Tim. "That is Mr. Whitcomb's number!"

Tiny Tim was born Herbert Khaury in 1932 in New York, the son of Tillie, a Jewish dressmaker from Brest-Litovsk, and Butros, a sweater knitter from Lebanon. He loved his parents, but on weekends they had screaming fights about money, so he retreated into thoughts of fairy tales and beautiful girls. The soundtrack to his Wonderland was provided by radio's *Your Hit Parade*, and Herbert sang along to both male and female singers, switching the vocal range accordingly. His father introduced him to the old, old songs by bringing him one day a 78 he'd picked up at a junk shop—a 1919 recording of Henry Burr singing "Beautiful Ohio," a sweet waltz.

From there, he took the long trail backwards to the very dawn of commercial recording, discovering other acoustic pioneers such as Byron G. Harlan and Ada Jones and, in particular, Irving Kaufman. The latter had a moral warning number, "Stay Home Little Girl," begging the country maiden not to be drawn like a moth to a flame by the sinful ways of big city men. Sin and its attraction were constantly in Herbert's mind and this record became an obsession. He'd lie on his bed, turn off the lights, pull down the shades, and play his 78 records, scratchy and bumpy as they were, over and over on the windup phonograph, sometimes stroking the horn in gratitude. While Kaufman provided the proper conduct lesson, Rudy Vallée's voice spread a welcome sexual unction, and Nick Lucas finished off the trip with his pretty picture of a luxuriant garden where the pixilated lover, knee-deep in tulips, tiptoed to heaven.

These 1920s crooners had the high-voice requirement of the era and Herbert seemed to be only able to emulate them by going into falsetto. This made him seem effeminate, but his parents encouraged him to sing at family gatherings and were relieved that he adored baseball. However, his mother grew alarmed when Herbert grew his hair too long and started wearing makeup. In the 1950s, beefcake, personified by stars like Marlon Brando in tight T-shirt and jeans, was the macho ideal. Herbert's deviation from the norm was dangerous. Even males who wore red shirts on a Thursday were suspect. It was a sexually very insecure age.

In 1950, Arthur Godfrey, as we know, brought the ukulele back into massive circulation. Herbert was so taken by Mr. Godfrey—he attached titles of courtesy to everybody—he attended the live radio shows religiously until he was thrown out for jumping up and down and clapping in the wrong places. He stayed at home from here on and learned to play the plastic Maccaferri Islander endorsed by Godfrey, with the aid of a method book cowritten by the star. Next he bought a Favilla at $25, a mighty sum for a uke. Now he was ready to go out and make something of himself. There were immense obstacles, the main one being himself.

He auditioned for Broadway shows, for off-Broadway shows, for any shows—but always got rejected. In order to avoid the humiliating walk to pick up one's music from the pianist, Herbert auditioned with his uke so that, upon rejection, he could beat a fast retreat. He didn't even have to take time putting the uke back in its case because he used a paper shopping bag and so—presto!—he was gone and on to the next rejection. He was always entering amateur talent contests. Ted Mack, who had a national show, remembered: "On at least four or five different occasions, a slight, persistent young man auditioned for our staff and each time was rejected. Well, we take consolation in the fact that we're not the only ones to have said 'no' to Tiny Tim."

Finally, in 1959, Herbert got a gig. True, it was at the bottom of the showbiz pit, almost as low as playing toilets, but he was a pro—he got paid. Hubert's Dime Museum & Flea Circus was the last surviving freak show, a line that had begun on New York's Bowery in the late nineteenth century and had actually provided a starting point for such vaudeville stars as Weber and Fields. In Herbert Khaury's case, he was the perfect fit and didn't really need to move on. As Larry Love, "the Human Canary," he shared billing with Sealo, who sported flippers rather than arms; Albert-Alberta, the Living Hermaphrodite; the Elephant Skin Girl; and, of course, Prof. Heckler and his World-Famous Trained Fleas at the very back of the penny arcade basement that housed the museum.

A few years later Herbert graduated to better gigs, to the proliferating folk and comedy clubs in and around Greenwich Village. This step up and his future progress were brought about by a series of managers. The trouble was that Larry Love, or Darry Dove or Judas K. Foxglove (some of the many stage names he gave himself), had an unfortunate habit of signing every piece of paper placed in front of them (him). He was a sweet fellow and did anything to oblige. By the time of his great breakthrough, he had contracts up to his neck. With the help of the managers, he played among the folkies at

Cafe Bizarre, Cafe Wha, the Ratfink Room, and Page Three. He loved Page Three, a lesbian club. He felt safe—and, at thirty, he had his first romance: Miss Snooky, who smoked cigarettes through a gap in her front teeth. He awarded her his first trophy, something he did for all the future "classic" beauties he was to encounter.

By this time he was Tiny Tim. His first manager, George King, was responsible for the final name change. In those pre-British Invasion days, before the stream of common Brit boys with gutter accents, "Merry Olde England," as I have said earlier, was regarded as a jewel house of aristocrats with diamond-cut accents. Herbert had taken to using the moniker "Sir Stafford Kripps," but this turned out to be too close to the real Sir Stafford (I was at school with the British politician's son) and so manager King dubbed his client Sir Timothy Tims and dressed him in top hat and spats. But Sir Timothy was unable to master the upper class accent and so King decided on "Tiny Tim." Easier to book, he reasoned.

So in December 1965, while I was fading as a teen idol and longing for my uke record to be released, Tiny Tim landed a terrific break. The Scene, away from and above the Village clubs, was the "in" spot for the young people—rock fans, not folkies. Here on the main stage, Tiny and his uke did "Tiptoe Through the Tulips" and other Alley novelties in the high voice and had the place howling. But his heart and soul were in the back room where, after hours, with head back, chin out, and eyes rolling heavenwards, he'd render Irving Kaufman's "Stay Home Little Girl" or Henry Burr's "Just a Baby's Prayer at Twilight."

Celebrities heard the buzz about Tiny and they dropped by the main stage for kicks and a laugh. Some of them collapsed in paroxysms of hysteria. The ballads, though, left them cold. Sincerity was not what they were after. Tiny was put on display at swell parties where were the happening people. He was viewed by Leonard Bernstein and Mick Jagger, men who were fascinated by the weird and in particular by the seemingly "ambisextrous" (I know: I had been grilled backstage by Jagger on the subject of my falsetto "You Turn Me On" a few months earlier). Bob Dylan invited him to his Woodstock refuge and there in a vast and empty room Tiny sang "Like a Rolling Stone" in the Rudy Vallée style followed by the crooner's "My Time Is Your Time" in the Dylan voice. The famous protest singer-cum-rock star offered him a banana and, none the wiser but culturally better informed, went to bed.

Eventually the record industry became interested. Richard Perry, an independent producer and arranger, was truly taken by Tiny and, with his own money and playing all the instruments himself, cut a few tracks. "April Showers," on which Tiny sings in his maiden aunt voice as well as doing a Jolson imitation, was the best and was released as a single on the Blue Cat label in 1966 when the vaudeville revival was in full swing. No dice. The next year Perry got lucky with a big label, Warner Bros. Records, and was asked to produce an album. This would become the best-selling *God Bless Tiny Tim* with the hit single "Tiptoe Through The Tulips."

Perry let Tiny play a little uke on the album but mostly supported him with L.A.'s top session men. This was particularly successful on "Then I'd Be Satisfied with Life," an obscure—even to vintage music aficionados—George M. Cohan specialty from the turn of the century,

Tiny Tim in all his splendor.
From the collection of Flea market Music.

now arranged in country style with pedal steel guitar and a few new lyrics: Tiny's preference for wheat germ, a breakfast dish, was listed as well as his adoration of Tuesday Weld, a one-time movie nymphet. Nico, a collaborator of the Velvet Underground—an Andy Warhol venture—stood in for Weld by breathily interpolating "I love you, Tiny!" A 1930s Maurice Chevalier vehicle, "Livin' in the Sunlight" was reinterpreted by Tiny and Perry to emerge as a new creation. This was not nostalgia, never tongue in cheek; this was original pop music and Perry was rightly proud of his work.

Television appearances obtained by his new high-powered management in collaboration with the Warner promotion department, however, were what made Tiny Tim the sensation of the nation—for a short while. On *Rowan & Martin's Laugh-In*, a smarty boots show, Tiny produced his uke from the paper bag—with faux stunned looks and mugging to the camera by the clever hosts—and sang sincerely. More appeals to the audience from the comics as if to say, "We have a creature here who is cuckoo, not playing with a full deck."

He hit the jackpot with his appearances on *The Tonight Show*. Johnny Carson, in his guise as the regular guy from the Midwest, knew to treat a freak with utter seriousness and, like Rowan and Martin, to register "Can you believe this?" takes to the audience. Viewers were stunned but clamored for more. Adults might shake their heads, but they wanted to goggle again at this antidote to the nightly news litany of Vietnam death and destruction. Teenage girls were crazy about him, a fairy-tale character, a vampire with no blood lust. So Tiny became a regular guest on *The Tonight Show*, eventually getting married on the show, as Wendell Hall had been married

on the radio back in the 1920s. But who the hell remembered Hall in the up-to-the-minute-forget-the-past 1960s? John Wayne knelt at his feet in homage. Princess Margaret fingered his uke. *Time* magazine, wise in this crass period of rock pretentiousness and cultural amnesia, concluded, "He is not imitating a vanished America. He IS that America."

Unfortunately, the TV people saw him as a flash in the pan to be exploited and then passed on as "yesterday's headlines"—the words used to his managers by *The Tonight Show* bookers in the early 1970s, when showbiz had moved on to new phenomena.

He never wavered, though, in his love of the old music and his wish to spread its happiness abroad. When Warner Bros. Records dropped him, he started his own label. When he couldn't fill the big venues, he played wherever he was invited. He defended the old songs against all comers: if audiences jeered the patriotic World War I songs, he shouted back at them. He'd even fought with Richard Perry about recording "America, I Love You," because Perry didn't want to have anything to do with flag-waving stuff at a time when the kids were demonstrating against the Vietnam War. In 1974, there were newspaper stories with headlines like "Whatever Happened to Tiny Tim?" and "Forgotten Tiny Tim Hits Comeback Trail."

Peace was found for Tiny in the desert near Palm Springs, the day he visited his hero Irving Kaufman. As the sun set, they sat on a couch and, to Tiny's uke accompaniment, they duetted "Stay Home Little Girl" and then cried together. Rudy Vallée became his friend; Gene Austin confided secrets concerning "My Blue Heaven"; Henry Burr was long dead.

His first bride, Miss Vicky, abandoned

him early; in 1984 he married Miss Jan, but they lived mostly apart; in 1995 he married Miss Sue. She was with him in September 1996 when he had a heart attack and fell off the stage at a concert for the Ukulele Hall of Fame in Massachusetts. Miss Sue had to help her husband, frail and not taking his heart pills, up the stairs of the Women's Club of Minneapolis on November 30 for an appearance. There'd been a muck-up on timing—guests were leaving— and the bandleader was hostile and claimed he knew nothing from the Tiny Tim repertoire. So Tiny and his uke performed alone. During "Tiptoe" he went all peculiar. Miss Sue asked if he was okay? "No, I'm not okay," he said and those were his last words.

In 1968 I saw Tiny Tim's success as an impediment to my uke career. I had already bought a $350 Martin soprano at Wallich's Music City in Hollywood. The original pawnshop Ukie was given to a friend and has since disappeared. I was intent on beginning a journey backwards to recover my roots—a rich past of both American and British popular songs and, in the ferment of a neophiliac rock culture that I disliked and felt alienated by, to present old trove as fresh and relevant and even commercial. My managers thought I was mad. Tower Records did not renew my contract.

When Tiny Tim hit big, I was put out of the picture as far as mainline showbiz was concerned. My work permit had expired, my star had faded; I crawled back to my family home in London and considered what next I should do. I hadn't the skills to be a clerk and there were few mines left to go down.

Then one evening I went to the Royal Albert Hall for Tiny Tim's triumphant concert. The Royal Albert Hall! He'd made it to the hal-lowed hall and I'd only made the Hollywood Bowl and then as part of a package show in July 1965. Here was Tiny Tim alone onstage except for a swollen orchestra conducted by Richard Perry in a white tie and tails. Elton John slid into a back row. I wondered if we'd be in for a freak show. I was still uneducated, Tiny-wise.

It was a most joyful, noble, and musical evening. He presented the same library of old and forgotten songs that I loved, and I was converted. The audience was respectful but celebratory, as if they were at a classical concert flooded with sugary light with hobbits flying around dispensing happiness. We sang along, we waved imaginary cigarette lighters.

In the years to come, I followed my backwards trail and Tiny Tim went out of my mind. But in writing this book, I knew I'd have to face him and seek his heroic aspects even though his looks were not godlike and his habits unappealing. It's the work and the spirit that must be studied: I have played his best records again and again, marveling at the mixture of musicology, creativity and, well, joie de vivre.

I have reappraised his art and decided that Tiny's a true Hero of the Ukulele, a sorcerer pointing a crooked but wise finger at America's unrecognized meat-and-potatoes-plus-ketchup pop. For the music of Tin Pan Alley and vaudeville is essential to the story of American music, alongside (but separate from) jazz and blues. Tiny called it "white man's soul."

His Albert Hall concert was a one-off—his music, my music—was that of the troubadour and best heard in unaffected locations: a dim café, a restaurant corner, a front room or a back porch. He wanted to spread his enthusiasm liberally, like the thickest peanut butter on the toast of our hearts.

CHAPTER SEVEN

OUR GREAT REVIVAL

NOT FORGETTING ROY SMECK, LYLE RITZ, AND THE UKULELE ORCHESTRA OF GREAT BRITAIN

In 1969, exiled back in my homeland, I got myself signed by Allen Lane, the hardback imprint of Penguin Books, to write a history of pop music from rag to rock. The subject needed a book; I also knew that this was the only way my story could ever get into print. Working at the dining room table of my mother's London flat I finished *After the Ball* in three years.

An early hit from Ian's Tin Pan Alley heroes, Edgar Leslie and Harry Warren.
From the collection of Ian Whitcomb.

primitive reel-to-reel video camera (see it on YouTube).

Turned on by my research into ragtime, Tin Pan Alley, and crooners, and fed up with being sedentary, I talked United Artists Records into letting me make an album called *Under the Ragtime Moon.* Neil Innes, late of the Bonzo Dog Doo-Dah Band and soon to be a Monty Python songwriter, produced and we had a splendid time peppered with much hilarity and tempered by an underlying purpose: we were celebrating ragtime as an effervescent song and dance.

The album was released in America in 1973 and I flew back to my land of dreams to promote, with Ukie—in hard-shell case as opposed to paper shopping bag—at my side. I saw ragtime as the rock 'n' roll of the early twentieth century. A revival might act as an antidote to the woes of our times.

Alas, my timing was off: the thinking and erstwhile chattering classes were talking in hushed and reverent tones about an album of Scott Joplin rags performed by classically trained Joshua Rifkin in a slow and stately style reeking of high seriousness. Articles mushroomed about tragic Joplin as a composer who might have taken ragtime into the realms of classical music had the action-shunning artist not been strangled by the crass pop music industry of the 1910s.

Here was I, a one-hit wonder in search of a bandwagon, trying to resurrect the clang-bang Tin Pan Alley. "Real ragtime," they said, was serious piano music for the concert hall and not an Alexander's Band bashing out a dance beat that might have folks turkey-trotting and throwing their arms in the air ejaculating, "It's

During the writing, I'd popped over to New York to get firsthand stories from veteran Alleymen such as Edgar Leslie and he'd put me in touch with his 1920s partner Harry Warren. So I flew on to Los Angeles and spent pleasant hours with Harry in his backyard office. To Edgar's lyrics he'd composed one of my all-time favorites, "Pasadena," and now he volunteered to sing along by supplying what he called the "obbligato" part, an old vaudeville trick. Ukie was there and Harry approved the harmonies. A friend caught the precious moment on my

a bear!" Such strictures had been leveled at me since prep-school days when the piano mistress had ordered me not to tap my foot, when the head of my dormitory had taken me to the headmaster's study for a caning because I was always singing silly pop songs.

However, I had a persistent publicist who managed to get me and Ukie booked on *The Tonight Show* on the strength of *After the Ball*, which had just been published by Simon & Schuster to good notices, even in *The New Yorker*, a creamy center of all that was sophisticated. "Brash, learned, funny, and perspicacious," they called me. Gosh, was I comforted!

In retrospect I'm amazed that Johnny Carson let me on his show in spring of 1974, seeing as how Tiny Tim was only allowed one final appearance that fall and then only as part of a group in what was termed a "charity booking." Why had Carson agreed to yet another retro uke entertainer and one who had no weirdness to support him? Maybe he liked my book.

The talent co-coordinator warned me on the morning of the show that his boss was uneasy with disabilities and that my stutter must therefore be suppressed at all costs. The answer was Valium, truly a miracle drug. I popped two tablets and became extremely garrulous, couldn't stop talking, haven't stopped since, and was ready to be shot from a gun when my name was announced by Carson that afternoon at the taping.

A close friend said I resembled a startled rabbit moments before execution as, in blue velvet jacket and bell-bottom trousers, I rushed through the curtain gripping Ukie as if he were the only defense from death. I sang "Hungry Women," a comedy song from the late 1920s, fast and furiously with much popping of the

eyes. Ukie, in contrast, was calm and carried on regardless.

Johnny Carson must have approved, because over the next few years I was booked several times. Laden with not only Ukie but also a vintage banjo-uke as yet unnamed, I once sang "Baby Your Mother (Like She Babied You)," from 1927 and a favorite of Tiny Tim's. The house band, led by Doc Severinsen, backed me with a genuine period arrangement I had given them. They played stylishly and authentically, never going hokey or corny. This was because at rehearsal Mr. Severinsen had stopped them from making stilted fun of the arrangement. "Play with respect," he told them quietly but firmly. "This music has a certain integrity." I'll always be grateful to him for that speech.

Mr. Carson, treating me with courtesy, was ever ready to cast a camera look of bewilderment to the folks at home if I grew boring or didn't make sense. The only rough ride I had was when Carson was away and John Davidson, a handsome middle-of-the-road singer with perfect blown and frozen hair, was guest host. I sang "Dance and Grow Thin" (Irving Berlin, 1917), rather well I felt. But when I took my place on the couch, he leaned across the desk, shook his head, and said, "You're not playing with a full deck."

Still, Ukie and I had made our mark on TV in an era when the ukulele was certainly not in vogue, and there were to be further guest shots on Merv Griffin's show—where I played a beautiful Martin *tiple*—as well as early morning slots on *The Today Show*. By this time, the late 1970s when disco was spinning its factory-made riffs and slogans, I had another album release, one that featured Ukie much more than on the ragtime excursion.

Ian on *The Tonight Show*
with Johnny Carson.
Photo by George Sherlock.

Derek Taylor, my onetime Hollywood publicist, was now in charge of Warner Bros. Records in London and, being a kind and eccentric soul, he ordered the release of *Ian Whitcomb's Red Hot Blue Heaven*, initially bankrolled by Ray Davies's label Konk. Ray, free from the Kinks and filling up on his British music hall heritage, was particularly fond of "My Girl's Pussy" (1930), although he also liked "The Farmyard Cabaret" (1932), where I made various animal noises.

None of my records were hits—those days were over, I guessed. I was plowing a lonely furrow, but I kept right on till the end of the road, as the old Harry Lauder song encouraged—the one Winston Churchill had hummed all through the war. There were books and TV shots and ragtime festivals; I was finally awarded the coveted green card, making me a resident alien, because I had proved that, as a ukulele player, I was taking no work away from Americans. Indeed, the official who handed me the card commented that I was probably the only professional uke player in the country. "Good luck, sir—you'll need it!"

In 1979 I bought a 1940s house in leafy Altadena, hard by the San Gabriel Mountains, under twenty miles from Hollywood and the action. I bought more Martin ukes but they were soon stolen, plus my tiple. Ukie, living under the bed, stayed safe. Lodgers were acquired so that my "home," as they call a house in America, would be occupied while I made forays into foreign countries (I now saw England as alien). In 1982, I made what almost amounted to a World Tour.

At the famous Montreux Jazz Festival in Switzerland with my ragtime pianist partner Professor Dick Zimmerman, plus Ukie, our trio made such a splash playing on the terrace by the lake that we were invited to join the televised evening concert—quite an honor. We were to open for Art Blakey & the Jazz Messengers, a modern ensemble. They had demanded a Bösendorfer grand piano, tops in its line. We presented Cliff Edwards's "Halfway to Heaven" and Irving Kaufman's "Who's Sorry Now?," piano ringing righteously and ukulele nicely percussive, and our international audience of jazz aficionados thoroughly bewildered.

Then I announced that Professor Zimmerman would perform a classic rag, "Pork and Beans." I left the stage to Dick who immediately made short work of the Bösendorfer. He's what's called a "forte pianist" and takes out his frustrations on innocent keyboards. In the wings, the French piano technician threw up his hands in horror at what Dick was doing to his precious instrument. The piano was indeed shaking and threatening to slide off the stage at any moment. "*Qu'est-ce que c'est?*" asked the technician. "Ragtime!" I said. "*Quelle horreur!*" said the man. The Art Blakey band followed our act. They reaped the results of the professor's merciless assault: the Bösendorfer was so out-of-tune that the Blakey pianist's modernistic chord substitutions sounded like good-time jangle piano at its best.

Undeterred, we moved on to Surfer's Paradise in Australia for more ragtime and ukulele propagandizing. The former colony reminded me of what Britain used to be like in the friendly 1950s, everybody cheerful with chins up and much backslapping. We were at a backyard party with beer cans spurting in a ballet (almost) synchronized to my interpretation of "I'm the Husband of the Wife of Mr. Wu" when the guest of honor, a dark man with a stick through his nose and ear lobes pulled low by the weight of enormous gold rings, caught my eye with a wave of his spear.

As chief of a tribe from an island between Australia and Tasmania, he was over there for a fund-raiser. Our host Bruce explained that once a year the tribe goes on a rampage, setting fire to their homes and businesses in a gesture against the white man. Next they fly to the mainland for a whip-round of the hat to pay for the damage. After my song, the chief approached and, as he idly tossed another jumbo shrimp on the barbecue, congratulated me on my performance, adding that he'd known all the words since childhood and that George Formby was one of the good things exported by the British Empire. Just as I was on the point of thanking him, he prodded me in the chest and asked whether I was aware that the ukulele had been invented on his very island. I threw some coins into the chief's proffered hat.

In London there were no concerts, but we did wangle a radio broadcast at Bush House for the BBC World Service. Fortunately there was no piano for Dick to destroy. We delivered our standard lecture on ragtime as America's first musical form and then I was asked to do a song. I obliged with "He Played His Ukulele as the Ship Went Down," a 1930s Jack Hylton comedy song. We got an angry tele-

gram from a merchant seaman of my acquaintance stating that while his ship was rounding the horn and the crew were tuned to the BBC for news of the Falklands War, then in full swing, all he and his mates could hear was me and that damned ukulele.

ROY SMECK

In New York, a better place for me and my work, I managed a week's engagement at Michael's Pub, a venue favored by Mel Tormé and Woody Allen. A friend said that the great Roy Smeck was still very much alive and living nearby. Now Smeck, "the Wizard of the Strings," had been a vaudeville, radio, and record star of the 1920s and '30s. He was an instrumentalist and never sang—but he was a virtuoso on guitar, banjo,

From the collection of Flea Market Music.

From the collection of
Flea Market Music.

Mills FAVORITES
for
UKULELE

Arranged by
ROY SMECK

*Complete Instructions
including tuning,
strumming, chords
for playing your
favorites.*

Contents

JEALOUS
WHEN YOU'RE SMILING
LONESOME AND SORRY
DIGA DIGA DOO
THE SHEIK OF ARABY
MA (He's Making Eyes At Me)
SENTIMENTAL GENTLEMAN
FROM GEORGIA
GOODBYE MY LADY LOVE
HOW COME YOU DO ME LIKE
YOU DO
BILLY
LET A SMILE BE YOUR UMBRELLA
and other favorites

Price
60¢

MILLS MUSIC, INC. • 1619 Broadway • New York 19, N.Y.

A Roy Smeck song collection.
From the collection of Flea Market Music.

and lap steel. Johnny Marvin's record of "12th Street Rag" had fired him up to learn ukulele and to best Marvin with the Smeck version. In vaudeville, he was famous for playing the uke upside down or like a violin, for spinning it and blowing down the sound hole and making train imitations, while keeping a fixed smile all through the clever stage business.

Still smiling as he played up a storm, Smeck starred in an early sound short made by Warner Bros. using their Vitaphone system. The Harmony Company produced a special Vita-Uke with the Roy Smeck signature, and he loved stopping off at any music store he happened upon to give a free demonstration. His method books poured out of the presses. In 1933, he was featured in a Russ Columbo picture called *That Goes Double* where, on a screen divided into a pie of four equal parts, Smeck was seen to play with himself on lap steel, banjo, guitar, and ukulele all at the same time. He topped this by doing his act that same year at President Franklin D. Roosevelt's inaugural ball. What a man!

He agreed to see me in his apartment. A sprightly and twinkly-eyed octogenarian, he was enthroned on a high chair in a yellow-lit corner of a big and empty room with a court of guitars and ukuleles fanned out in front of him. At his request Ukie and I performed. His eyes grew even brighter as if lit by a sudden revelation. "Aha!" he said. "You are only a *strummer*."

He demanded that I hand him my uke. He twisted the strings higher and higher till he achieved a brittle ring. "If you're gonna be in vaudeville, then you gotta have a bright sound to keep the people's attention, see?" He proceeded to enthrall me with a seated version of his old act including the celebrated tap dance routine—on the front and back of poor Ukie. I thanked him and left.

That night at the club all four strings snapped during my act. As ukuleles were not exactly hip at the time, I had to ask around for a place where strings could be bought. There was only one store, they said, and it was a long way away and down an unsavory alley. When at last I arrived there, the sullen man at the counter said that, yes, he had uke strings but there was not much demand for them anymore. He pulled out a few dusty packets. They were all brand-marked "Roy Smeck."

I've since wondered whether Smeck's sideline was ensnaring uke players in order to break

Courtesy of The Ukulele Orchestra of Great Britain.

OUR GREAT REVIVAL

their strings and thus propagate his name. He certainly deserved to be better known.

THE UKULELE ORCHESTRA OF GREAT BRITAIN

A few years later I returned to London to plug *Irving Berlin & Ragtime America*, my new biography of the great man. This gave me a chance to appear on a BBC TV magazine program and present one of my new songs, "You've Got to Show It to Mother." After the broadcast I was thrilled to take a call from the secretary of the George Formby Society. He sounded just like George, really thick North Country. It was hard to follow him. I did catch a query about whether it was hard to play upside down. "Easy," I said. "I'm like Tiny Tim." The line went dead.

At a publisher's launch party at Pizza Express, I actually did sing a few Berlin numbers with Ukie. A thirteen-year-old boy was standing near and watching me intently. Will Grove-White, the son of celebrated author and advice columnist Virginia Ironside, later said the experience of watching me inspired him to take up the uke. By this time he was a fully fledged member of the Ukulele Orchestra of Great Britain.

I caught their act a couple of years after Will had caught mine. I'd lent the boy one of Ukie's brothers, another Martin. He went and left it on the tube (the London Underground electric train) and felt terrible. I told me not to worry even though I was grieving. His mother Virginia took him to see the Ukes when they were in their infancy, around 1987, and playing at Ronnie Scott's Club, a murky but hip basement in London's Soho. The place was packed and there was a picnic party atmosphere, very un-showbizzy, maybe folk-whimsical. The Ukes

bravely interpreted Wagner and Tchaikovsky and Charlie Parker, boiling the music down to its essentials: melody, harmony, and rhythm. What music is all about. Four strings multiplied by eight players told the truth—and so a rottenly made tune was easily exposed as nonsense. They were pretension detectives. Deconstruction in the best way. I liked that, having been always suspicious of classical music with its stiff concerts of bulbous sawing string frippery, of penguin-suited players, of ludicrous conductors waving their arms pointlessly.

From European classical warhorses (made pony-lively), they dove into Chuck Berry sung lugubriously. There was no George Formby or Billy "Uke" Scott. I was sorry about that. And a bit fearful lest I crash head-on with the orchestra bosses.

Virginia Ironside, ever the matchmaker, arranged a dinner party at her house for me to meet George Hinchliffe and Kitty Lux, founders of the Ukulele Orchestra of Great Britain. Virginia advised me to be careful with my loose tongue since George and Kitty might be a little left-wing. Luckily we got on like a house on fire and, if anything, I found them delightfully anarchist and game for a world with no rules and an openness to all music. In fact, I almost suggested they consider adding such songs of mine as "You've Got to Show It to Mother" or "Wurzel Fudge the Village Idiot" to their repertoire. But wisely, and aided by a kick under the dinner table from Virginia, I desisted.

After plum pudding and as the port decanter and cigars went 'round, George told me that he and Kitty had coined the term "Ukulele Orchestra" knowing it had a touch of irony, rather like "the Gobi Desert Scuba Diving Club," but that from this early fun conceit they

Will Grove-White, George Hinchcliffe, and Ian at Will's mother's London flat rehearsing for a concert—early 1990s.

were determined to "sixteen-handedly turn the world on to the possibilities of the ukulele" and eventually tour the world "carrying only hand luggage." Meanwhile, they were playing the humbler venues and George was making ends meet with his evening gig tinkling cocktail piano in a country pub.

Will Grove-White had joined the Ukes by this time and now invited me to be their guest at Cecil Sharp House, the headquarters of the British folk music movement. They backed me on my comic songs and seemed to get a kick out of it. I didn't bring up the Formby name—I had a feeling that the Ukes' audience was a million miles from Blackpool, tripe, and cowheels. I felt

a waft of French cheeses and white wines.

But I had made my bed on the West Coast and had to run back there soonest. The Ukes and I and went our separate ways. In 1990, I was married to the lovely cooking and singing Regina. With a voice like a lark and a keen sense of what was best, she steered me in the direction of Great American Songbook numbers by Jerome Kern and George Gershwin.

She also tried to steer me away from any future confrontations like the one in the San Francisco underground parking lot. I had gotten into a standoff for a parking space with a long black limousine and its menacing driver. As the latter advanced I raised Ukie, who, naturally, was in his hard-shell case. Aiming the case at my adversary I said, "I warn you—I am fully armed!" The man backed away with many apologies and much doffing of his black cap.

Meanwhile the Ukes were building a repertoire of clever material and a classy act that enabled them eventually to play the Royal Albert Hall, the Sydney Opera House and, in the new century, Carnegie Hall. All instant sellouts. Old Beatles and Monty Pythons were fans. Quality newspapers praised and analyzed. *The Daily Telegraph* noted their use of the ukulele as a fine "bullshit detector." So popular had they become in Britain by 2007 that they spawned hundreds of ukulele orchestras named after hometowns, villages, universities, and prisons. So popular had they made the instrument that a national shortage was declared in the Isles that year and emergency shipments had to be ordered from China.

I have stayed in touch. George Hinchliffe, the begetter, knew I was writing this book and though admitting to a toleration of Formby's "Leaning on a Lamp-Post"—providing it's deconstructed and then reconstructed in a minor key with Russian echoes—he is marching to a different drum from me. Of course, we remain friends and admire each other's work. For this book he kindly provided a paragraph describing the mission of the Ukes:

The Ukes espouse a low-tech aesthetic, even an anarchistic anticorporate stance. The fake and the foolish are targets hit fair and square by the apparently gentle, dry humor of the orchestra.

Well put, George!

Based in my Altadena home, anchored by my wife Regina and guarded by Inspector, an old dog we had inherited from Rudy Vallée (Tiny's hero and mine, too), I continued to play my ukulele whenever conditions were right: live on my radio show at Pasadena's KPCC, an NPR affiliate; in concert at the annual 1920s festival held near an artificial lake on the grounds of the Workman & Temple Rancho and Homestead in the unlikely location of the City of Industry; on recordings made in a local garage for my own label, ITW Records.

The uke was still a hard sell, a piece of ridiculousness to so many, a position largely created by the Tiny Tim fallout. Upon telling a hip or thinking person that I played uke, the inevitable response was a sardonic impression of "Tiptoe."

But one lazy Sunday afternoon in 1992, through the good offices of my longtime friend and editor Ms. Ronny Schiff, I was visited by an extraordinary ukulele visionary, a tall and thick-haired chap full of crusading zeal yet without any born-again silliness: Jim Beloff, late of the East Coast and now working locally for *Billboard* as associate publisher, wanted to meet and greet both me and Ukie.

Proudly he showed me the vintage Martin tenor uke he'd recently spotted lying on a ratty blanket at the Pasadena Rose Bowl Flea Market. That's why he was starting a company called Flea Market Music, that's why he intended to publish songbooks with sophisticated arrangements like the ones in the old Ukulele Ike books. Maybe there'd be concerts in the future where players would gather and give praise. They may be around here; they *must* be around. If not we'll conjure them up, I added, catching some of Jim's spirit. We will raise the ukulele from the dead!

He certainly had raised my flagging sprits.

Courtesy of The Ukulele Orchestra of Great Britain.

I had been too long out alone in the cold. He and his wife Liz soon became our friends.

Next year *Jumpin' Jim's Ukulele Favorites*, artfully designed by Liz, appeared and was distributed by the world's number-one music publisher, Hal Leonard. Clearly Jim was on the right track, steered by his business acumen and training. The content ranged from early Alley sing-along standards to "Over the Rainbow." I supplied a picture of Ukulele Ike in a beanie. Tiny Tim was represented by "Tiptoe." The chord grids were large and simple and correct.

More books followed in a flurry of themes—Christmas, Hawai'i, Hollywood, and a *'60s Uke-In* with a handwritten appreciation from George Harrison:

It is one instrument you can't play and not laugh! It's so sweet and also very old . . . Everyone I know who is into the ukulele is crackers, so get yourself a few and enjoy yourselves.

Harrison had spent an afternoon in 1999 at Jim's house. On entering, the first thing he did, even before proper introductions were made, was to grab a banjo-uke from the wall and launch into "Leaning on a Lamp-Post" in the Formby style. Then, settling down into what he'd been invited there for, he inspected the uke collection, seventy of them. Jim was by now a self-confessed sufferer from UAS (Ukulele Acquisition Syndrome). George was no novice or Johnny-come-lately. Paul McCartney has spoken of how the after-dinner ritual at the Harrison house wasn't brandy and cigars, but instead was the bringing-on of the ukes. All guests were expected to play together. And if they couldn't play, then George would instruct. Rock stars tell of being there on innocent social visits and getting forced into day-long lessons conducted by George, so ardently that their hands were aching by cocktail time. At the end of the evening they'd be led to a parked car, one of many. Amazingly, the trunk of this one was packed to the gills with ukes of many kinds and sizes. The guest would be told to take a few with him or her. "You never know when you might be caught short without one," said their host.

The Beloff uke books, especially the method one, were selling well, but many of the customers expressed frustration at the scarcity of classic ukes and the absence of a decent reasonably priced new one. Jim saw a market and encouraged his engineer brother-in-law Dale Webb to design what became the Fluke, a ukulele shaped like a balalaika and made from injection-molded thermo-plastic plus a little wood for humanity's sake.

I bought one—much to Ukie's chagrin—because the Fluke was not only tuneful but also sturdy and loud. Therefore I could take it on rough-and-ready gigs and swing it about, even bash it, and no harm done. Ukie by this time was getting on in years and had a tendency to splinter when I was in the overexcited vein.

Ukie had been hospitalized many times at McCabe's Guitar Shop in Santa Monica. The repairman, John Zehnder, expressed concern. He'd never seen such abuse before. Flukie was young and healthy and strong. But even he had trouble with my flaying nail on his top string. Bing! It would break so many times at my shows, while Ukie in his younger days had never flinched. Engineer Webb was puzzled and took it upon himself to solve the mystery. Flukie was flown east, where Webb examined the patient carefully at his workshop. After sculpting the end of the fret board near the slash lines of my

Jim Beloff with Fluke in hand.
Photo by Aaron Kotowski, from the
collection of Flea Market Music.

brutal strums, Flukie was sent home and has troubled me no longer.

Jim's promise of uke concerts was realized in August 1999, with the first proper UKEtopia™ held at folksy McCabe's. Jim had his new and splendid coffee-table book, *The Ukulele: A Visual History* for sale, as well as breezy-bright real Hawaiian shirts. I offered my recently published contribution to the songbook library, *Ukulele Heaven*, containing "Where Did Robinson Crusoe Go?" as well as my latest compositions, "The Uke Is on the March" and "Ukulele Heaven." The sales objects sat between plates of health-conscious cookies and fruit juices. No taint of burgers and beer. I felt certain that our audience, gentle souls of a liberal persuasion, would display a love of sandals. After all it was August.

My journal records that I was very excited to be on the bill. "I love being part of a team—no longer alone!" We'd had a sort of dry run the year before: the *Legends of Ukulele* concert was a way of alerting people to Jim's Rhino Records CD of the same name, a compilation of ukesters ranging from Ukulele Ike and George Formby to Tiny Tim and myself and Jim.

Now the West Coast revival was starting to catch fire, the customer line went round the block, and the players came from the north and south of California. There were teenage Andy Powers, a whiz instrumentalist from San Diego, and Ukulele Dick, comedian of the strings, from Santa Cruz. There was Janet Klein of Hollywood, glamorous reviver of "obscure, naughty, and lovely songs of the 1910s, '20s and '30s"; and Rick Cunha, grandson of Sonny Cunha (father of the "hapa haole" song) providing lap steel guitar; and Fred Sokolow, author of countless stringed instrument instruction books, playing guitar to fill out the sound.

LYLE RITZ

In time for the concert and just in from Hawai'i, where he'd been in a sort of retirement, was Lyle Ritz, master of the jazz ukulele. In the 1950s, as a jazz bass player schooled by Stan Kenton alumni, he'd fallen in love with the uke, in his case the bigger sound of a Gibson tenor. Verve Records, the well-respected jazz label started by Norman Granz, commissioned him to record two albums on what was still considered a novelty or toy, despite Arthur Godfrey's crusading. So dazzlingly musical were these LPs that a new generation of Hawaiian ukulele players emerged, deeply influenced by this genial fellow whose magic fingers were resurrecting the uke for jazz ears, taking it away from lei-garlanded tourists.

I knew Lyle from the rocking 1960s when he'd been an in-demand bass player, part of the legendary "Wrecking Crew" of studio session men playing behind the Beach Boys, the Righteous Brothers, and Sonny & Cher—and you name them. Well, I will: Lyle backed me on several of my "Turn On" rock follow-ups that never made the charts, but are at least quite musical thanks to himself and other Crew members such as guitarist James Burton and saxist Jim Horn.

My wife, Regina, and I were the penultimate act, duetting on the old ballad "Let the Rest of the World Go By." This was followed by the finale, the high point of the evening, when Jim, our MC, invited everyone to bring out his or her uke. Jim reckoned rightly that our audience had been itching for an invitation to play. Rather than break the spell with the passing-out of music sheets, the Beloffs had come up with a much better idea: As the mighty string band played "Aloha 'Oe," Liz Beloff and Regina, together with the Chordateers, a bunch of little kids, held up cardboard blowups of chord grids, changing them to the appropriate one under Liz's direction. A train wreck was thus avoided.

There's nothing like the sound of massed ukuleles—bagpipes be damned. I found the experience quite moving—everybody in accord. In fact I had a rare moment of speechlessness. Head swimming in the juice of ecstasy, I came downstairs from the artists' upper floor to greet the fans—I mean, my fellow ukesters. A woman approached and introduced herself as George Harrison's sister-in-law. Fascinating. But then: "George has some of your records." Amazing. "Just a minute," I said—and pulled from my briefcase a clutch of my latest CDs, plus the new songbook. She backed off as I presented them: "He likes your stuff—but not that much!"

Attending UKEtopia™ were executives and crew from a movie that several of us had recently worked on: *Stanley's Gig*, starring William (*Blade Runner*) Sanderson as an "emotionally dysfunctional minstrel with a big dream to play his ukulele on a cruise ship line to Hawai'i," coupled with Faye Dunaway as his lady friend. Jim Beloff and I had songs in the film, Fred Sokolow led the band, and the soundtrack was recorded at Rick Cunha's garage studio. Since Sanderson was neither a singer nor a uke player, I was called upon to dub both his voice and his strumming. Borrowing from Arthur Godfrey, I wrote myself into the script as "Smiling Jack," a radio personality who decades ago taught uke on the air. Long dead, Jack now gives moral courage to our hero Stanley in moments of stress. My song "Ukulele Heaven" became the opening and closing music. It was a noble indie, produced and directed by young men, and the first (and only) full-length feature film to center on a ukulele player. The *New York Times* gave a decent review. It won all kinds of festival prizes and has played around the world on TV for years.

UKEtopia™ became an annual event and, in a possibly unrelated act of God synchronism, ukulele clubs and festivals began sprouting on our West Coast. The most vivacious and vociferous group (not an organization, because they take pride in being disorganized) was (and is) the Ukulele Club of Santa Cruz, with hundreds of members and still counting.

Carrying on the sixties' hippie rule-flaunting tradition, the club has no rules (except that every performer has to get a standing ovation) and no ruler. The cofounder's official title is "Not Sure Why I'm President," and his partner's slogan is "The uke is inclusive and certainly not exclusive."

So it's "Free-for-All Hall" when they meet each month. You are at sea bobbing about with a million happy people, all fully armed and ready to fire. I never saw so many ukes, so many makes, so many custom-made, or homemade from cigar boxes or preserved and toughened pineapple.

Every member can have his or her say whenever. Such freedom makes it often hard to get a word in edgeways, especially if you're that month's guest act. You try to perform, but you're drowned out by the merry company doing their own especial thing. This is truly democracy at work and I love it.

My applause when I play for them—although few have properly heard me—is overwhelming, and there are always members who will ply me with Jack Daniel's shots coupled with the beer of my choice.

In 2004 the club actually organized an

Lyle Ritz in the late 1950s.
From the collection of Flea Market Music.

Hawaiian Hotel in Waikiki in 1927; he taught Shirley Temple and Clark Gable to strum; and he provided the uke playing on Bing Crosby's hit record "Blue Hawaii". At UkeFest he showed off his extraordinary and most melodic technique before trading jazz licks in a friendly cutting contest with Lyle Ritz.

As MC I couldn't get them off the stage, but then why should I? There are no rules in Santa Cruz, so I gazed out to sea and relaxed with a strong tiki cocktail. The president came up to ask whether I'd like to join the club in a few months' time at their "Burning Uke" celebration: a giant ukulele, high as a kite, would be set on fire deep in some forest away out over the mountains. He promised dancing around the conflagration followed by a jam session. I politely but firmly demurred. Like George Harrison's limited appreciation of my CDs, I am a uke fan but only to a certain extent.

A year or so later, down the coast, I was MC at a more stately event—a bit of an eye- and ear-opener. Orange County, reputedly staid and conservative, was to be the site of a ukulele festival heavy with actual Hawaiians, now living together on the mainland. I was rather surprised to have been invited, since musically I'd been bred in the opposite direction of the isles. I soon realized I'd have to watch my p's and q's, for the exiles took their music seriously and were quick to point out that the "ook-oo-laylee"

event called UkeFest West—blissful days in a beachfront pleasure palace crammed with the best players of the time and all appearing for free. I was master of ceremonies, if you could call it that. The Kings of Misrule really ran the event. But I did get to meet and introduce Bill Tapia, a nonagenarian ukester from the golden age of Hawaiian hapa haole, an associate of Sonny Cunha. He had played in the Johnny Noble Band at the historic opening night of the Royal

"UKEtopia"™ on stage at McCabe's in Santa Monica, California. L–R: John Zehnder, Chuck Fayne, Travis Harrelson, Shep Stern, Jim Beloff, Bergman Broome, Ian Whitcomb, Janet Klein, Peter Brooke-Turner (from The Ukulele Orchestra of Great Britain), Fred Sokolow, King Kukulele, Jeff Falkner, and Rick Cunha. Note that many in the audience are strumming along to instructions by the Chordateers.

From the collection of Flea Market Music.

(the correct Hawaiian pronunciation) was their native instrument, as were all things attached to it. This was all right with me because I've always adored all things Hawaiian, especially the food.

Both the music and dance—the hulas—were religious exercises of great antiquity and I pointed this out in my introductions. The young girls hip-shaking in short grass skirts may spur the blood, but the spectacle, please remember, is both spiritual and historical.

Less antique and delicate were bands of young mainlander Hawaiians with rock sensibilities pushing their strapping ukes through a cityscape of amplifiers and speakers, and altering their sound every moment by stepping on an array of foot pedals. This was the uke up-to-date and away with "Tiny Bubbles"! For decades, the uke had been seen as a kitsch relic of colonial days and vulgar tourists.

Some of the young Turks at the festival raved about a kid from O'ahu called Jake Shimabukuro, a virtuoso technician, star of a group called Colon. Deeply influenced by martial arts, he whirls a percussive strum in a hyper manner and can skip quick from an electrified "Star-Spangled Banner" à la Jimi Hendrix to Paganini's violin showpiece *Caprice No. 24*. Watch him take the world by storm, said the boys.

The Orange County Hawaiians were amused by and tolerant of my Alley songs. We all made room for each other. We had started a revival in the West on a coast reviled and despised and envied for having developed the dance band, the movies, rhythm and blues, surfboards, and fast food. We knew our time was coming. We knew the East would eventually catch up.

Meanwhile, in the new century, I have settled into my kind of uking, leading Ian Whitcomb & His Bungalow Boys and guesting with Janet Klein & Her Parlor Boys. My songbooks continue to pour out and I take the opportunity to join the communal activity in California. I love dropping in on an evening workshop at, say, Church of the Chimes in Sherman Oaks where meet each month the Jumpin' Flea Circus Players of Los Angeles. I marvel at the filled pews of ukesters, after a hard day's work in retail or rocket science, as they lean into their instruments, poring over chord grids to "California, Here I Come" or "Bridge over Troubled Water," singing along lustily or sweetly, watching their leader as he conducts from his uke.

The community bulletin board for that October tells me that Ukulele Bartt will be conducting a "half-day mega-workout" at the Coffee Gallery in Altadena, a short walk from my home and a week before Will Ryan leads his Royal Ukulele Band of Hollywood at the same venue. Will wants me to play "My Horse Likes Accordion Music" with the band but I'd rather play uke on a Cliff Edwards song.

Our Ukulele Heroes, from King Kalakaua and Frank Crumit to Arthur Godfrey and Tiny Tim, are to be admired and emulated. But the thrust of today's movement is populist and leaderless. It is all about singing and strumming together. The string theory—the ultimate unification of everything—sits on my lap embodied as Ukie. He has been through many ups and downs, but he's stayed loyal by staying in tune.

Now we sit together in my library at the back of the darkling garden where I began this book. Night approaches like a robber but I can still see with a saintly clearness—and an old vision returns. A vision that the fence in front of me is disintegrating and so are all the others for miles and miles ahead. The walls are tumbling down—I can hear them—and the bunkers and barracks and prisons are melting. The bottomless pit is being filled by something you'll like—I can hear that tune too.

And at last I can see them on the far horizon, marching along with ukes at slope arms, an astonishing army, ready to amaze the welkin. Our Heroes, in the backdrop, are smiling as they hear the anthem:

Spread the news nation to nation . . .
The uke is on the march!
Bringing our strummed syncopation . . .
The uke is on the march!
We don't moan our blues,
We don't holler or whine.
Our melodies jingle, our words even rhyme.
Step aside electronics . . .
Make way for Ukephonics™
The uke is on the march!

OUR GREAT REVIVAL

ACKNOWLEDGMENTS

Putting together my first book, *After the Ball: Pop Music from Rag to Rock*, took me three years. I was twenty-eight when I started. Writing this latest book took two and a bit months. I had just hit seventy when I started.

And I am worn out, but happy. I wrote in a white-hot fever, had ideas and whole sentences while walking or swimming or sleeping, had to jot or stab them down fast on scraps of paper, toilet roll strips, the business section of the newspaper . . .

Then I came out back to the hut I call my library and, tapping with the left-hand middle finger which is the one next to the strum finger which is next to the thumb, I put down this story on an old Apple Cube, which is not supposed to be still living.

I'm sorry the story is over. The work has been a labor of love and sweat, but no wailing and gnashing of teeth. The lack of frustration is thanks to the unstinting and immediate help from two pillars of the ukulele community: Jim Tranquada and Jim Beloff.

Right at the start, when I immediately got stuck in the Hawaiian chapter, Jim Tranquada, the expert, answered my questions on the phone and at dinner and then emailed any and all information he had on, say, the Portuguese who brought over the four-string model to the islands and the Hawaiians who perfected it and took it as a gift to the mainland. He went on to send rare stuff on Cliff Edwards, May Singhi Breen, and Johnny Marvin, and on and on. He was utterly unselfish, despite the fact that he has a new book published, a scholarly one, on the history of the ukulele.

Jim Beloff of Flea Market Music, the musician/businessman largely responsible for the current uke revival, begged me to be kind to Tiny Tim and mailed me a rare biography and fan magazine from Tim's period. He also provided me with material on Arthur Godfrey. Jim was always there at his East Coast telephone to answer my questions, to calm me down and tell me how much he likes my style. For this is a book of style and spirit.

Will Grove-White, whom I knew when he was a boy and whom I provided with his first ukulele, corrected and made suggestions for changes in the section about the band he's a member of—the Ukulele Orchestra of Great Britain. His boss George Hinchliffe sent me a quirky summary of the band's origins and aims—most of which I used.

Michael Daly, son of the late Kevin, who produced an LP of me for British Decca in the early 1970s, masterminds the best website devoted to George Formby. He went over my Formby chapter and made sure that wife Beryl was treated fairly. Unhesitatingly, he sent my editor lots of rare photos of George from his files.

And speaking of my editor: Ronny Schiff is also my friend, so it must have been hard for her to keep a balance. But I trust her completely: without her eagle eye and sensitive approach to my tendency to get carried away and go overboard, this book wouldn't have been the delicious, fast read it is. *I think*. Ronny initiated the project and steered it through the corporate stages. Of course she was dealing with some very nice people at the Hal Leonard organization, especially our editor and facilitator there, Mike Edison.

Finally, my long-suffering but loving wife, Regina, put up with my comings and goings from hut to house to the big Apple computer for hard copy of factual stuff, a crazed march that resulted in housekeeping going awry. I had neglected my domestic duties for the sake of some then-dubious art. She knew it was all for our future good, but eventually she became uke-nuked and wisely took a vacation in the snow up north. That was at Tiny Tim time, and she knew when enough was enough. She has always backed my work with common sense and uncommon affection and understanding. And you ought to hear her sing!

Oh, and not forgetting Rollo the Dog, who pawed at the library door every day when he was finished barking at squirrels. I'd let him in to curl up beside me as I tapped away. He wasn't there, though, the day I came in the library door and was confronted by a burglar in the act. "I just need food, man," he said. "I'm not interested in ukuleles."

Ian and Rollo.

POSTSCRIPT

To enhance your reading of this book, visit YouTube and type in all the Heroes' names. You'll be rewarded with clips from their movies, TV shows, and concerts, as well as their recordings. It's an amazing treasure trove—everyone appears to be there in this Internet pantheon and they seem to be staying.

So, sit back in your favorite chair with a choice drink at hand and look at our book while you listen to the sweet sounds of our Heroes.

SELECTED DISCOGRAPHY
CDS ONLY

JIM BELOFF

Jim's Dog Has Fleas. FMM R102

LIZ & JIM BELOFF

Rare Air. FMM R105

FRANK CRUMIT

Around the Corner. Conifer CDHD 174

Gay Caballero. Pro-Arte CDD 3407

CLIFF EDWARDS

Singing in the Rain. ACD 17

The Vintage Recordings of Cliff Edwards
(Ukulele Ike). TT4 19CD

GEORGE FORMBY

England's Famous Clown Prince of Song
(5 CD set). JSP Records JSP 1901

The War & Postwar Years (5 CD set). JSP 1902

ARTHUR GODFREY

The Old Redhead. Collector's Choice CCM 177 2

WILL GROVE-WHITE

Will Grove-White & The Others. willgrovewhite.com.

WENDELL HALL

*Vocalist's Showcase Vol. 13 Presenting Songs by
Wendell Hall*. Vintage-Recordings.com

HAWAI'I

John King: *Royal Hawaiian Music*.
Nula Music 002

Various Artists: *Hawaiian Memories*.
Take Two TT 506CD

**JANET KLEIN &
HER PARLOR BOYS**

Whoopee! Hey! Hey! — Songs to Cheer in Tumultuous Times. Coeur de Jeannette 0012

JOHNNY MARVIN

Breezin' Along with the Breeze.
Living Era CD AJA 5453

TESSIE O'SHEA

I'm Ready, I'm Willing. Pavilion Records Past
CD 7078

OVERVIEW

Legends of Ukulele. Rhino R2 75278

LYLE RITZ

Lyle Ritz—Time . . . Ukulele Jazz.
Flea Market Music FMM-R-109

Lyle Ritz—No Frills. Flea Market Music
FMM-R-113

LYLE RITZ/HERB OHTA

A Night of Ukulele Jazz, Live at McCabe's.
Flea Market Music FMM 1004

**WILL RYAN AND THE CACTUS
COUNTY COWBOYS**

The Outlaws Are Coming.
Audible Records WR 3737

JAKE SHIMABUKURO

Gently Weeps. Hitchhike Records HBCD 1105

Live. Hitchhike Records HBCD 1109

ROY SMECK

Hawaiian Guitar, Banjo,
Ukulele and Guitar 1926–1949. Yazoo 1052
Magic Ukulele of Roy Smeck.
Universal Distribution 9025

FRED SOKOLOW

The Night Owl.
Sokolowmusic.com

TINY TIM

Tiny Tim Live! At the Royal Albert Hall.
Rhino Handmade RHM2–7710
Resurrection. Bear Family Records BCD 15409

THE UKULELE ORCHESTRA OF GREAT BRITAIN

A Fist Full of Ukuleles. Sony SPCS 7412
The Secret of Life. Tom's Cabin BNCP 95

IAN WHITCOMB

I Love a Piano. Rivermont Records BSW 2218
Sentimentally Yours. ITW Records 011

UKULELE HEROES
THEIR TOP FIVE SONGS

FRANK CRUMIT

"Ukulele Lady"

"Mountain Greenery"

"Sweet Lady"

"Abdul Abulbul Amir"

"The Girl with the Paint on Her Face"

CLIFF EDWARDS (UKULELE IKE)

"Singin' in the Rain"

"Halfway to Heaven"

"It Had to Be You"

"A Pretty Girl Is Like a Melody"

"Losing You"

GEORGE FORMBY JR.

"Chinese Laundry Blues"

"The Window Cleaner"

"The Wigan Boat Express"

"Fanlight Fanny"

"Auntie Maggie's Remedy"

ARTHUR GODFREY

"Makin' Love Ukulele Style"

"Pale Potomac Moon"

"Bum-Deedle-Um-Bo"

"Too Fat Polka"

"When I Take My Sugar to Tea"

WENDELL HALL

"It Ain't Gonna Rain No Mo'"

"Paddlin' Madelin' Home"

"She's Still My Baby"

"Land of My Sunset Dreams"

"Meadowlark"

THE HAWAIIANS

"Aloha 'Oe"

"On the Beach at Waikiki"

"Hula Blues"

"Dear Old Honolulu"

"Song of the Islands"

JOHNNY MARVIN

"Oh, How She Could Play the Ukulele"

"From Midnight Till Dawn"

"Sweetheart of All My Dreams"

"12th Street Rag"

"Me and My Shadow"

TESSIE O'SHEA

"Two Ton Tessie (From Tennessee)"

"Nobody Loves a Fairy When She's Forty"

"You're at Blackpool by the Sea"

"It All Belongs to Me"

"Live and Let Live"

LYLE RITZ

"Lulu's Back in Town"

"No Moon at All"

"Ritz Cracker"

"I Love a Ukulele"

"Honolulu"

ROY SMECK

"Tiger Rag"

"My Mom"

"My Buddy"

"Melody in F"

"Humoresque"

TINY TIM

"Tiptoe Through the Tulips"
"Then I'd Be Satisfied with Life"
"Livin' in the Sunlight"
"April Showers"
"Great Balls of Fire"

IAN WHITCOMB

"Where Did Robinson Crusoe Go with Friday
  on Saturday Night?"
"Do I Love You? Yes, I Do!"
  (with Regina Whitcomb)
"Ukulele Heaven"
"The Uke Is on the March"
"My Dog Has Fleas"

SELECTED FILMOGRAPHY

CLIFF EDWARDS

The Hollywood Revue of 1929 (1929)

Dough Boys (1930)

Way Out West (1930)

Take a Chance (1933)

Cliff Edwards and His Musical Buckaroos (1940)

Pinocchio (1940)

Dumbo (1941)

Fighting Frontier (1943)

Fun and Fancy Free (1947)

The Man from Button Willow (1964)

GEORGE FORMBY

Boots! Boots! (1934)

Off the Dole (1935)

No Limit (1935)

Keep Fit (1938)

I See Ice (1938)

It's in the Air (1939)

Come On George! (1940)

Let George Do It (1940)

Turned Out Nice Again (1941)

George in Civvy Street (1946)

JOHNNY MARVIN

Sunny Side Up (1929)

Gold Mine in the Sky (1938)

Under Western Stars (1938)

Ride, Tenderfoot, Ride (1940)

TESSIE O'SHEA

Holidays with Pay (1948)

Somewhere in Politics (1949)

The Blue Lamp (1950)

The Russians Are Coming, the Russians Are Coming (1966)

Bedknobs and Broomsticks (1971)

LYLE RITZ

Bound for Glory (1976)

ROY SMECK

The Wizard of the Strings (1985)

TINY TIM

You Are What You Eat (1968)

IAN WHITCOMB

Stanley's Gig (2000)

VARIOUS ARTISTS

(including: Janet Klein, Robert Armstrong, Travis Harrelson, Ukefink, the Haoles, Pineapple Princess, Ian Whitcomb)

Rock That Uke (2003)

VARIOUS ARTISTS

(including: Jim and Liz Beloff, James Hill and Jake Shimabukuro, Jon Braman, John King, and more)

Mighty Uke (2010)

INDEX OF SONGS

INDEX